# THE
# GREEN
# SLOW COOKER
## COOKBOOK

# THE
# GREEN
# SLOW COOKER
# COOKBOOK

## 80 EASY AND DELICIOUS VEGAN AND VEGETARIAN MEALS

**SASKIA SIDEY AND LIBBY SILBERMANN**

hamlyn

# hamlyn

First published in Great Britain in 2024
by Hamlyn, an imprint of
Octopus Publishing Group Ltd,
Carmelite House,
50 Victoria Embankment,
London EC4Y 0DZ
www.octopusbooks.co.uk

An Hachette UK Company
www.hachette.co.uk

Some of this material previously appeared in *Vegetarian Slow
Cooker, Vegan Slow Cooker, Hamlyn All Colour: 200 Slow Cooker
Recipes, Hamlyn All Colour: 200 More Slow Cooker Recipes,
Hamlyn All Colour: Slow Cooker Recipes* and *Hamlyn All Colour:
200 Family Slow Cooker Recipes*.

Distributed in the US by Hachette Book Group,
1290 Avenue of the Americas, 4th and 5th Floors,
New York NY 10104

Distributed in Canada by Canadian Manda Group,
664 Annette Street, Toronto, Ontario,
Canada M6S 2C8

ISBN 978-0-600-63866-7

A CIP catalogue record for this book is available from the
British Library.

Printed and bound in China.

10 9 8 7 6 5 4 3 2 1

**Picture credits**
Octopus Publishing Group: Stephen Conroy 14, 11, 26, 55, 60, 110,
150, 156; Lis Parsons 25; William Shaw 6, 13, 17, 21, 29, 30, 33, 34,
37, 38, 41, 42, 47, 48, 51, 52, 56, 59, 63, 64, 67, 68, 71, 72, 75, 76, 79,
80, 83, 84, 87, 88, 91, 92, 95, 96, 99, 100, 103, 113, 114, 117, 118, 121,
122, 125, 126, 129, 130, 133, 134, 137, 138, 141, 142, 145, 146, 149, 155,
159, 160, 163, 164, 167, 168, 171, 175, 176, 177, 179, 180, 183, 184;
Eleanor Skans 18.

**Cookery notes**
Standard level spoon measurement are used in all recipes.
1 tablespoon = one 15 ml spoon
1 teaspoon = one 5 ml spoon

Both imperial and metric measurements have been given in all
recipes. Use one set of measurements only and not a mixture
of both.

Ovens should be preheated to the specific temperature – if using
a fan-assisted oven, follow manufacturer's instructions for
adjusting the time and the temperature.

Eggs should be medium unless otherwise stated.

Milk should be full fat unless otherwise stated.

Fresh herbs should be used unless otherwise stated. If
unavailable use dried herbs as an alternative but halve the
quantities stated.

Pepper should be freshly ground black pepper unless
otherwise stated.

This book includes dishes made with nuts and nut derivatives.

Vegetarians should look for the 'V' symbol on a cheese to ensure
it is made with vegetarian rennet.

# CONTENTS

# INTRODUCTION

A slow cooker is a brilliant alternative to oven cooking. You can leave it for many hours to cook away and do the work for you or use it as a tool to create impressive dinner party dishes. It is surprisingly versatile and often creates the optimum environment for low and slow cooking.

This book includes recipes that cover breakfast, light lunches, long and slow dinners and sweet treats – all updated and adapted to use the best vegan and vegetarian ingredients available.

Although the slow cooker will do the majority (if not all) of the work in most of these recipes, some recipes involve some extra steps for maximum flavour, such as frying, sautéing, roasting or grilling. Similarly, some dishes require finishing in the oven or under the grill. Slow cookers are increasing in popularity and, despite their association with slow-cooking meat, the recipes in this book will demonstrate the wide spectrum of meat-free dishes that are possible in your slow cooker. I hope it fills you with inspiration at the endless possibilities of wonderful, delicious and highly varied vegan and vegetarian dishes you can create in your slow cooker.

## A NOTE ON SLOW COOKER CAPACITY

All the recipes in this book were tested in a 6.5 litre (11½ pint) slow cooker, so adjust the quantities and cooking times according to the capacity of your slow cooker if necessary.

Take particular care with baking recipes: if using a 3.6 litre (6 pint) slow cooker, instead of baking the batter in a 900 g (2 lb) loaf tin where instructed, line the bottom and sides of the slow cooker pot with nonstick baking paper and add the batter directly; and for the Cherry Bakewell Breakfast Cake (see page 28) and PB & J French Toast Bake (see page 32), halve the ingredient quantities.

## SLOW COOKER TOP TIPS

Follow these simple guidelines to ensure successful slow cooking every time.

- **Less is more** If you're adapting one of your favourite recipes to be made in the slow cooker, be sure to reduce the liquid content by at least one-third, if not half. Because of the tight-fitting lid and prolonged cooking process, most of the liquid will not evaporate from a slow cooker, so you could end up with a thin, runny sauce. If this does happen, transfer the cooking liquid to a saucepan and simmer briskly, uncovered, on the hob until reduced, or remove 2 tablespoons of the cooking liquid and mix with 1 tablespoon of cornflour in a cup until smooth. Return to the pan and simmer for a few minutes, stirring, until thickened.

- **Layer flavours** Although a lot of the time it can be tempting to skip preliminary stages like sautéing onions and garlic, toasting spices or marinating vegetables, these steps will add deep flavour to your dishes. You can, of course, just throw all the ingredients into the slow cooker to cook, but you might end up with something a little less tasty.

- **Consider temperature** Be mindful of whether your ingredients are refrigerator-cold before going into the slow cooker – this will affect cooking times. Make sure any stock in the recipe is boiling hot before it's added or this will delay the cooking process. If you're in a hurry, preheat your slow cooker while you prep.

- **Keep greens fresh** Slow cooking some green vegetables can lead to them looking a bit brown and sludgy. Unless otherwise instructed, always add leafy green vegetables and fresh herbs at the last minute to keep things vibrant.

- **Put a lid on it (sometimes)** We always want to peek into our slow cooker to check on progress, but it's important to resist the urge, as opening the lid lets the carefully calibrated temperature of the slow cooker dip and can affect your dish. Each time you open the lid will add about 15 minutes to the cooking time. However, when baking certain dishes or attempting to reduce liquid in a dish, it's often advisable to place a tea towel or kitchen paper underneath the lid to trap the steam, or to position the lid slightly ajar for some of the cooking time to allow steam to escape, as directed where appropriate in the recipes.

- **Make cleaning up a breeze** Where possible, grease your slow cooker pot to avoid any stuck-on food at the end of the cooking process. When baking or cooking a very sticky mixture, line the pot with nonstick baking paper, or stock up on specially designed plastic slow cooker liners that can prevent burnt bottoms and crusty slow cooker pots.

- **Be flexible** Slow cooking is not the most intuitive way to cook and different models of slow cooker run at slightly different temperatures, so you have to keep a degree of flexibility with cooking times and get to know your own cooker. A recipe that says it takes 2 hours to cook could be ready in closer to half that time in some slow cookers.

- **Highs and lows** Most slow cookers have two functions: 'high' and 'low'. If you want to cook something for longer than stated, or need it on the table sooner, as a general rule of thumb it takes twice as long to cook something on low than on high. For example, if a recipe states 8 hours on low, you could cook it for 4 hours on high instead. It is also worth noting that power and temperature settings vary with different brands of slow cookers. Therefore, although all the cook times are accurate for the recipes in this book, it is worth checking your dishes from time to time as they cook.

- **Reheating and storing** Don't use your ceramic slow cooker pot to store leftovers, as it's designed to keep the contents warm for extended periods of time and can lead to harmful bacteria breeding. Similarly, do not use your slow cooker to reheat leftovers, as harmful bacteria can reproduce in the time it takes for the pot to heat up.

- **Prep like a pro** When preparing your ingredients, think carefully about the size you are cutting your vegetables into. Are you cooking on low for 10 hours? Make the pieces bigger so that they don't turn into mush. Need dinner on the table in 1 hour? Cut them as small as you can to ensure even cooking in a short space of time. Plan ahead certain recipes that you can prep for in advance – any that call for all ingredients just to be dropped into the slow cooker can be chopped and prepared, frozen in freezer bags, defrosted and then cooked straight away.

- **Timing is everything** A lot of slow cookers don't have built-in timers, so make sure you have one nearby for setting the cooking time because it's very easy to lose track of whatever you're cooking and ruin dinner!

- **Stay steady and safe** Make sure your slow cooker is on a secure flat surface away from anything flammable or delicate – the outside of the cooker can get very hot, so you need to be careful when handling it.

## VEGETARIAN INGREDIENTS

While you're probably well versed in buying vegetarian produce, here is a list of ingredients that can sometimes contain animal products. Always make sure you double check the label on the packaging before purchasing. There are, of course, vegetarian alternatives to all the following items, so you shouldn't run into any difficulty, but it's important to keep these in mind when shopping.

- **Cheese** Some traditional cheesemaking processes use animal rennet, which makes the product nonvegetarian. Make sure you buy cheese made with vegetarian rennet instead.

- **Pesto** Pesto often contains Parmesan cheese, which is made with animal rennet.

- **Wine** Wine can contain animal proteins that are used in the fermentation, clarifiying and fining processes, so always double check the label.

- **Worcestershire sauce** Non-vegetarian Worcestershire sauce traditionally contains anchovies.

- **Vinegar** Vinegar can contain animal proteins. Vegetarian vinegars are available but always double check the label. Alternatively, all distilled vinegars and malt vinegars are vegetarian, and acidic flavours such as lemon juice can also be used in their place.

## VEGAN INGREDIENTS

Certain ingredients can sometimes contain hidden animal products. Always make sure you double check the food label on the packaging before purchasing. There are, of course, vegan alternatives to all these items, but it's important to keep these in mind when shopping.

- **Bread** Some bread can contain milk or butter.

- **Chocolate** Vegan chocolate should be labelled as such, but look out for 'whey' or 'casein' on dark chocolate labels – don't assume that all 70% cocoa dark chocolate is dairy free.

- **Citrus fruit** The wax routinely found on citrus fruits such as lemons, limes and oranges contains shellac or beeswax, which are insect by-products, so buy unwaxed wherever possible.

- **Dairy-free cheese** Some dairy-free soya-based cheeses can still contain casein, so make sure you look for the vegan certification.

- **Icing sugar** This type of sugar can contain dried egg white, so double check the ingredients list.

- **Jam** Some jams contain gelatine as a thickener rather than the traditional (and vegan) pectin.

- **Margarine** While most margarines are made from vegetable fats, some can be blended with yogurt or contain other animal proteins, so make sure you check the label carefully.

- **Pre-packaged foods** Even if a product is vegetable based – vegetable soup, for example – it can sometimes contain milk powders or egg as a thickener. Double check condiments such as pesto, barbecue sauce and bottled salad dressings.

- **Vinegar** Vinegar can contain animal proteins. Vegan vinegars are available but always double check the label. Alternatively, acidic flavours such as lemon juice can also be used in their place.

- **Wine, cider & beer** These items can contain animal proteins, used in the fermentation, clarifiying and fining processes, so always double check the label.

- **Worcestershire sauce** Non-vegan Worcestershire sauce traditionally contains anchovies.

## KEY TO RECIPE SYMBOLS

**VEGETARIAN**

**VEGAN**

# BREAKFAST CLUB

**MAKES 2 KG (4 LB)**
Preparation time 5 minutes, plus standing and fermenting
Cooking time 2½ hours

# BIO-CULTURED YOGURT

2 litres (3½ pints) milk
100 g (3½ oz) natural live yogurt
   (check the packaging for
   live cultures)
vanilla bean paste or honey
   (optional)
blackberries, blueberries and
   halved cherries, to serve
   (optional)

Pour the milk into the slow cooker, cover with the lid and cook on low for 2½ hours. Turn off the cooker and leave to stand with the lid on for 3 hours.

Ladle 500 ml (17 fl oz) of the warm milk into a large bowl, add the yogurt and whisk together until smooth. Return the mixture to the slow cooker and stir well, then replace the lid. Wrap the slow cooker in a large towel so it is well insulated (this creates a good environment for the yogurt cultures to become active). Leave to ferment, without lifting the lid, for 8 hours until set and ready to use.

Transfer to an airtight container and store in the refrigerator for up to 2 weeks. To continue culturing your own yogurt, reserve 100 ml (3½ fl oz) from this batch to use as your starter for the next.

Mix the yogurt with a little vanilla bean paste or honey, if liked, before serving with blackberries, blueberries and halved cherries, or you could try other chopped fruit, such as mango, peach, raspberries or banana. This yogurt is also delicious served on Honey, Nut & Seed Granola (see page 16), Salted Maple Granola (see page 36) or in little pots on top of Fruit Compote (see page 23).

**SERVES 4**
**Preparation time 5 minutes**
**Cooking time 4 hours**

# SLOW COOKER CREAMY PORRIDGE

100 g (3½ oz) jumbo oats
500 ml (17 fl oz) milk or
    400 ml (14 fl oz) can coconut
    milk mixed with 100 ml
    (3½ fl oz) water
1 teaspoon ground cinnamon
    (optional)

*To serve (optional)*
light or dark muscovado sugar
sliced banana

Put the oats and milk into the slow cooker and stir well. Add the cinnamon, if using, cover with the lid and cook on low for 4 hours until the porridge has reached your desired consistency.

Serve just as it is or with your choice of topping – try a sprinkle of light or dark muscovado sugar and some sliced banana.

**MAKES 12 SERVINGS**
Preparation time 10 minutes, plus cooling
Cooking time 2½ hours

# HONEY, NUT & SEED GRANOLA

350 g (11½ oz) jumbo oats

100 g (3½ oz) coconut flakes

50 g (2 oz) sunflower seeds

50 g (2 oz) raw almonds, chopped

50 g (2 oz) walnuts, chopped

1 teaspoon ground cinnamon

4 tablespoons coconut oil, melted

175 g (6 oz) clear honey or agave syrup

50 ml (2 fl oz) water

1 teaspoon vanilla extract

125 g (4 oz) raisins

50 g (2 oz) dried cranberries

*To serve (optional)*

shop-bought yogurt or homemade yogurt (see page 12)

fresh berries

milk of your choice

Put the oats, coconut flakes, seeds, nuts and cinnamon into the slow cooker and mix well.

Mix together the coconut oil, honey or agave syrup, measured water and vanilla extract in a small bowl, then pour this over the oat mixture and stir until well combined.

Cover with the lid at a slight angle so there is a small gap to allow the steam to escape (this will help the granola to crisp), then cook on high for 2½ hours, stirring gently every 40 minutes to ensure the mixture is not sticking to the pot or burning.

Carefully remove the slow cooker pot from the cooker using oven gloves, then carefully tip the granola onto a large baking tray and spread it out evenly. Leave to cool (this ensures it will be crunchy), then stir in the raisins and cranberries. Store in an airtight container for up to 2 weeks.

Serve the granola with yogurt and fresh berries, or simply with your milk of choice.

SERVES 4
**Preparation time 15 minutes, plus overnight soaking**
**Cooking time 4 hours**

# BLUEBERRY & CINNAMON FRENCH TOAST

**50 g (2 oz) butter, softened, plus extra for greasing**
**1 teaspoon ground cinnamon**
**150 g (5 oz) soft brown sugar, plus extra for sprinkling**
**8 slices of bread, slightly stale**
**1 teaspoon vanilla bean paste**
**pinch of sea salt**
**3 large eggs**
**300 ml (½ pint) milk**
**100 g (3½ oz) blueberries, plus extra to serve**

*To serve (optional)*
**natural Greek yogurt**
**clear honey**

Beat together the butter, cinnamon and sugar in a small bowl until it forms a smooth paste, then carefully spread each slice of bread with the butter mixture on both sides.

Whisk together the vanilla bean paste, salt, eggs and milk in a large, shallow dish until smooth. Place the slices of bread into the egg mixture, ensuring each slice is submerged. Cover the dish with clingfilm and place in the refrigerator overnight.

When ready to cook, grease the slow cooker pot well with butter. Arrange a layer of the soaked bread slices in the bottom of the pot. Sprinkle over a layer of blueberries, then add another layer of bread. Repeat until all the bread and blueberries are used, then pour over any remaining egg mixture and sprinkle the top with sugar.

Cover with the lid and cook on low for 4 hours until the egg mixture has thickened and set. Carefully remove the slow cooker pot from the cooker using oven gloves. Cut the French toast into slices and serve with extra blueberries and dollops of Greek yogurt and a drizzle of clear honey, if liked.

**SERVES 4**
**Preparation time 10 minutes**
**Cooking time 5 hours 20 minutes**

# SHAKSHUKA

1 onion, finely sliced

3 garlic cloves, crushed

460 g (14¾ oz) jar roasted red
    peppers, drained and sliced

300 g (10 oz) mixed-colour
    cherry tomatoes, chopped

2 x 400 g (13 oz) cans
    chopped tomatoes

2 tablespoons tomato purée

1 teaspoon smoked paprika

1 teaspoon ground cumin

1 teaspoon dried oregano

4 large eggs

50 g (2 oz) feta cheese

10 g (¼ oz) fresh coriander,
    chopped, to garnish

*To serve*

pitta breads or flatbreads

natural yogurt

Put the onion, garlic, red peppers, fresh and canned tomatoes, tomato purée, paprika, cumin and oregano into the slow cooker and mix together. Cover with the lid and cook on low for 5 hours until tender and full of flavour.

Make 4 wells in the surface of the mixture, then carefully crack an egg into each well and crumble over the feta cheese. Replace the lid and cook on high for about 15–20 minutes until the egg whites are set but the yolks are still runny.

Meanwhile, toast the pitta breads or flatbreads, or warm them through in a preheated oven according to the packet instructions.

Divide the eggs and tomato mixture between 4 serving dishes and sprinkle with the chopped coriander. Serve with dollops of yogurt and the toasted pitta breads or flatbreads.

SERVES 4
Preparation time 10 minutes
Cooking time 2½–3½ hours

# FRUIT COMPOTE

300 g (10 oz) cranberries
500 g (1 lb) red plums, quartered
 and stoned
200 g (7 oz) red seedless
 grapes, halved
4 teaspoons cornflour
300 ml (½ pint) red grape juice
100 g (3½ oz) caster sugar
1 cinnamon stick, halved
pared rind of 1 small orange

Put the cranberries, plums and grapes into the slow cooker pot.

Mix the cornflour with a little of the grape juice in a bowl until smooth, then stir in the remaining juice. Pour into the slow cooker pot and add the sugar, cinnamon and orange rind.

Stir together, then cover with the lid and cook on low for 2½–3½ hours or until the fruit is tender.

Serve warm or cold, with thick, creamy yogurt (see page 12) or stirred through porridge (see page 15). The compote can also be served with cream as a dessert.

**SERVES 4**
Preparation time 45 minutes
Cooking time 2 hours

# SWEET POTATO, GOATS' CHEESE & THYME FRITTATA

2 sweet potatoes, about 625 g
   (1¼ lb) in total, peeled and
   cut into bite-sized pieces
2 tablespoons olive oil, plus
   extra for greasing
1 onion, finely sliced
3 garlic cloves, finely sliced
6 large eggs
1 tablespoon thyme,
   leaves picked
50 g (2 oz) soft goats' cheese
salt and pepper

Preheat the oven to 200°C (400°F), Gas Mark 6. Put the sweet potatoes on a baking tray. Drizzle with 1 tablespoon of the oil, then season well with salt and pepper and toss until well coated. Roast for 25–30 minutes until tender and lightly golden brown.

Meanwhile, heat the remaining oil in a frying pan, add the onion and fry over a medium-low heat for 5 minutes until soft and translucent, then stir in the garlic and cook for 3 minutes until the onion and garlic are lightly golden.

Grease the slow cooker pot well with oil, then add the onion mixture and roasted sweet potatoes and mix until combined. Beat together the eggs in a large bowl. Add the thyme leaves, crumble in the goats' cheese and season well, then pour the egg mixture over the sweet potatoes.

Cover with a lid and cook on low for 2 hours until the eggs are set and a skewer inserted into the frittata comes out clean. Carefully remove the slow cooker pot from the cooker using oven gloves. Loosen the edge of the frittata with a knife and turn out onto a large plate. Cut the frittata into slices and serve warm, or store in the refrigerator for up to 3 days, to serve cold on another occasion.

**SERVES 4**
Preparation time 5 minutes
Cooking time 8–10 hours or overnight

# VANILLA BREAKFAST PRUNES & FIGS

1 breakfast tea teabag
600 ml (1 pint) boiling water
150 g (5 oz) pitted prunes
150 g (5 oz) dried figs
75 g (3 oz) caster sugar
1 teaspoon vanilla extract
pared rind of ½ orange

*To serve*
natural yogurt
muesli

Put the teabag into a jug or teapot, add the boiling water and leave to soak for 2–3 minutes. Remove the teabag and pour the tea into the slow cooker pot.

Add the whole prunes and figs, the sugar and vanilla extract to the hot tea, sprinkle with the orange rind and mix together. Cover with the lid and cook on low for 8–10 hours or overnight.

Serve hot with spoonfuls of natural yogurt and a sprinkling of muesli.

MAKES 6–8 SLICES
**Preparation time 15 minutes**
**Cooking time 1–1½ hours**

# CHERRY BAKEWELL BREAKFAST CAKE

70 ml (2½ fl oz) melted coconut,
    vegetable or sunflower oil
200 ml (7 fl oz) unsweetened
    almond milk
finely grated zest and juice of
    1 unwaxed lemon
120 ml (4 fl oz) maple syrup
1 teaspoon vanilla bean paste
½ teaspoon salt
150 g (5 oz) ground almonds
150 g (5 oz) self-raising flour
½ teaspoon bicarbonate of soda
½ teaspoon baking powder
150 g (5 oz) dried cherries
20 g (¾ oz) flaked almonds

*To serve (optional)*
dairy-free yogurt
cherry jam

Line the bottom of the slow cooker pot with nonstick baking paper so that it comes at least 2 cm (¾ inch) up the sides.

Whisk together the oil, almond milk, lemon zest and juice, maple syrup, vanilla bean paste, salt and ground almonds in a large bowl until well combined. Sift in the flour, bicarbonate of soda and baking powder and fold in gently. Add in three-quarters of the dried cherries and fold in gently.

Pour the batter into the slow cooker and spread it out evenly. Sprinkle the flaked almonds and remaining cherries on top.

Place a tea towel or kitchen paper underneath the slow cooker lid, cover the cooker and bake on high for 1–1½ hours until springy but firm to the touch and very lightly golden.

Remove the pot from the slow cooker and leave the cake to cool in the pot slightly. Then use the lining paper to lift the cake out of the pot and leave to cool on a wire rack. Serve warm, with some dairy-free yogurt and a dollop of cherry jam if you like, or leave to cool completely. Store in an airtight container for up to 4 days.

MAKES 6–8 SMALL OR 5–6 LARGE MUFFINS
Preparation time 15 minutes, plus standing
Cooking time 1½ hours

# BLUEBERRY MUFFINS

vegan butter, for greasing
(optional)
125 ml (4 fl oz) dairy-free milk,
such as soya or almond milk
½ teaspoon apple cider vinegar
2 tablespoons sunflower or
vegetable oil
½ teaspoon vanilla bean paste
175 g (6 oz) plain flour
75 g (3 oz) caster sugar
1½ teaspoons baking powder
1 teaspoon bicarbonate of soda
½ teaspoon salt
finely grated zest of
1 unwaxed lemon
125 g (4 oz) fresh or
frozen blueberries

Put 8 silicone fairy cake cases or 6 silicone muffin cases (or 5 or 6 greased mini pudding tins, depending on how many fit) into the slow cooker pot.

Mix together the dairy-free milk and vinegar in a bowl and leave to curdle for about 10 minutes.

Add the oil and vanilla bean paste and whisk together until well combined.

Mix together all the remaining ingredients, except the blueberries, in a separate large bowl. Then gradually fold in the dairy-free milk mixture and blueberries until well combined.

Add approximately 2 tablespoons of batter to each fairy cake case or muffin case or pudding tin. Place a tea towel or kitchen paper underneath the slow cooker lid, cover the cooker and cook on high for 1½ hours until the muffins are domed and firm to the touch.

Remove from the slow cooker and serve warm, or leave to cool completely on a wire rack. Store in an airtight container for up to 5 days.

**SERVES 4**
Preparation time 15 minutes, plus standing
Cooking time 1–1½ hours

# PB & J FRENCH TOAST BAKE

½ tablespoon sunflower or
   vegetable oil, for greasing
2 tablespoons ground
   flaxseed (linseed)
50 g (2 oz) vegan butter, melted
200 ml (7 fl oz) unsweetened
   almond milk
3 tablespoons smooth
   peanut butter
½ teaspoon ground cinnamon
¼ teaspoon ground nutmeg
½ teaspoon baking powder
250 g (8 oz) stale sourdough,
   cut into large cubes

*To serve*
icing sugar
3 tablespoons jam of
   your choice
roasted, unsalted peanuts,
   roughly chopped

Grease the slow cooker pot with the oil.

Put the ground flaxseed, melted vegan butter, almond milk, peanut butter and spices into the slow cooker, then use a whisk to break up the peanut butter and whisk until the mixture is emulsifed. Leave to stand for 5–10 minutes until slightly thickened.

Stir in the baking powder, add the bread cubes and toss until well coated in the mixture.

Place a tea towel or kitchen paper underneath the slow cooker lid, cover the cooker and cook on high for 1–1½ hours until springy but firm to the touch and the remaining liquid is thickened, golden and bubbly.

Serve immediately, dusted with icing sugar, drizzled with jam and scattered with chopped roasted peanuts.

**SERVES 2–3**
Preparation time 5 minutes
Cooking time 4–6 hours

# OVERNIGHT TURMERIC PORRIDGE

100 g (3½ oz) rolled oats
700 ml (1¼ pints) almond, soya
   or light coconut milk
2 teaspoons ground
   turmeric (optional)
2 tablespoons demerara sugar
1 teaspoon vanilla bean paste
pinch of salt

*To serve*
sliced mango
pomegranate seeds
toasted coconut flakes
maple syrup (optional)

Put all the ingredients into the slow cooker, cover with the lid and cook on low for 4–6 hours. If your slow cooker has the function to switch over automatically to 'keep warm' once the cooking time is up, leave to cook overnight. Alternatively, set a separate timer to make sure the porridge doesn't overcook and burn.

Give the porridge a good stir before serving, as it will probably have a slight crust on top. Loosen with a dash of water or extra dairy-free milk if it seems dry.

Serve warm, topped with sliced mango, pomegranate seeds and toasted coconut flakes, and drizzled with maple syrup if you like.

MAKES ONE 1 LITRE (1¾ PINT) JAR
Preparation time 10 minutes, plus cooling
Cooking time 2–2½ hours

# SALTED MAPLE GRANOLA

100 g (3½ oz) coconut oil or
   vegan butter, melted
400 g (13 oz) rolled oats
50 ml (2 fl oz) maple syrup
100 g (3½ oz) unsalted nuts,
   such as almonds, pecans or
   walnuts, or a mixture, kept
   whole or roughly chopped
25 g (1 oz) mixed seeds, such
   as flaxseed (linseed), pumpkin
   and sunflower
1 tablespoon sea salt flakes
½ teaspoon vanilla bean paste
½ teaspoon ground cinnamon
100 g (3½ oz) dried fruit, such
   as raisins, dried cherries,
   dried cranberries or roughly
   chopped dried apricots

Grease the slow cooker pot with 1 teaspoon of the coconut oil or
melted vegan butter.

Mix together all the remaining ingredients, except the dried fruit,
in a large bowl until well combined.

Transfer the granola mixture to the slow cooker and cover with the
lid but position it slightly ajar. Cook on high for 2–2½ hours until
the mixture is golden and crunchy. Stir 2–3 times during the cooking
time to make sure the granola isn't catching on the bottom, but don't
be too vigorous so that you keep big clusters of the mixture.

Stir the dried fruit through the granola. Transfer to a tray, spread
out and leave to cool completely and crisp up further. Store in a
clean airtight jar for up to 2 weeks.

**SERVES 4**
Preparation time 15 minutes, plus pressing
Cooking time 2 hours

# TOFU TOMATO BREAKFAST DIP

2 tablespoons extra virgin
   olive oil
1 onion, finely chopped
400 g (13 oz) can chopped
   tomatoes
2–3 roasted red peppers from
   a jar, drained and chopped
2 garlic cloves, thinly sliced
1 teaspoon ground cumin
1 teaspoon cayenne pepper
1 teaspoon sweet paprika
350 g (11½ oz) firm tofu
salt and pepper

*To serve*
1 avocado, sliced
small handful of fresh coriander
   and flat leaf parsley, chopped
dried chilli flakes
flatbreads, warmed

Put 1 tablespoon of the oil, the onion, tomatoes, red peppers, garlic and spices into the slow cooker and toss until well combined. Season to taste with salt and pepper. Cover with the lid and cook on high for 2 hours until the mixture is slightly reduced. Check and adjust the seasoning.

Meanwhile, drain the tofu well, sit on a sheet of kitchen paper and top with a second piece of kitchen paper. Place a heavy bowl or chopping board on top and leave to press for 20–30 minutes, replacing the sheets of kitchen paper if or when they become oversaturated in liquid.

Preheat the oven to 200°C (400°F), Gas Mark 6. Cut the tofu into 2.5 cm (1 inch) cubes, toss with the remaining tablespoon of oil and season with salt and pepper. Spread out on a baking tray and roast in the oven for 25–30 minutes until golden and crispy.

Serve the tomato sauce topped with the roasted tofu and sliced avocado, sprinkled with the chopped herbs and a few chilli flakes, with the warm flatbreads on the side.

SERVES 8
Preparation time 15 minutes
Cooking time 8 hours

# 'REFRIED' BEAN WRAPS

2 tablespoons olive oil

1 onion, finely chopped

3 garlic cloves, finely chopped
or crushed

450 g (14½ oz) dried pinto beans

1.4 litres (2½ pints) hot
vegetable stock

2 teaspoons ground cumin

1 teaspoon chilli powder

½ teaspoon dried oregano

juice of 1 lime

salt and pepper

*To serve*

tortilla wraps

mashed avocado

tomato salsa

lime wedges

fresh coriander sprigs

Put all the main ingredients, except the lime juice, into the slow cooker with 2 teaspoons of salt, cover with the lid and cook on low for 8 hours until the beans are tender.

Reserve a mugful of the cooking liquid, then drain the beans and use a potato masher to mash the mixture to a chunky purée or use an immersion blender to blend until smooth. Season with the lime juice and additional salt and pepper to taste. Add a little of the reserved cooking liquid if you prefer a looser consistency (the bean mixture will thicken as it cools).

Serve warm on tortilla wraps, with the mashed avocado, tomato salsa, lime wedges and coriander sprigs served alongside, for everyone to help themselves.

**SERVES 4**
**Preparation time 15 minutes**
**Cooking time 5 hours**

# SMOKY BREAKFAST BEANS

1 tablespoon olive oil

1 onion, finely sliced

3 garlic cloves, crushed

400 g (13 oz) can haricot beans,
    drained

300 g (10 oz) passata
    (sieved tomatoes)

1 tablespoon tomato purée

1 bay leaf

20 g (¾ oz) soft brown sugar

1 teaspoon smoked paprika

1 tablespoon apple cider vinegar

handful of parsley, chopped,
    to garnish

vegan buttered toast, to serve

Heat the oil in a frying pan, add the onion and fry over a medium-low heat for 5 minutes until soft and translucent. Stir in the garlic and fry for 3 minutes until the onion and garlic are lightly golden.

Transfer the onion mixture to the slow cooker, then add the remaining ingredients and mix together until well combined.

Cover with the lid and cook on low for 5 hours until the sauce has thickened and the beans are soft. Alternatively, cook on high for 3 hours.

Serve the beans piled on to vegan buttered toast, sprinkled with the chopped parsley.

# MAINS: 3½ HOURS OR LESS

**SERVES 4**
Preparation time 25 minutes
Cooking time 3 hours

# PEA & WATERCRESS SOUP

1 tablespoon olive oil
1 onion, chopped
2 celery sticks, chopped
3 garlic cloves, chopped
1 large potato, peeled
    and chopped
1 litre (1¾ pints) vegetable stock
400 g (13 oz) frozen peas
200 g (7 oz) watercress
salt and pepper

*To serve*
100 g (3½ oz) crème fraiche
small handful of cooked
    peas (optional)
small handful of pea
    shoots (optional)

Heat the oil in a frying pan, add the onion and celery and fry over a medium heat for 5 minutes until softened, then stir in the garlic and fry for 3 minutes until softened.

Transfer the onion mixture to the slow cooker, add the potato and pour in the stock. Cover with the lid and cook on high for 2½ hours.

Stir in the frozen peas and watercress, replace the lid and cook, still on high, for a further 20 minutes until the vegetables are tender and cooked through.

Turn off the slow cooker and leave to cool slightly, then purée the soup while still in the slow cooker pot using a stick blender. Alternatively, carefully transfer the soup to a blender and blend, in batches if necessary, until smooth, then return to the slow cooker.

Season to taste with salt and pepper. Cook the soup on high for a further 10 minutes, to warm through.

Ladle into bowls and top with swirls of the crème fraiche, a good grinding of pepper and a few cooked peas and pea shoot sprigs, if liked.

SERVES 4
Preparation time 20 minutes
Cooking time 2½ hours

# MUSHROOM PEARL BARLEY RISOTTO

2 tablespoons olive oil, plus
  extra to serve
1 onion, finely chopped
1 leek, trimmed, cleaned and
  finely chopped
4 garlic cloves, crushed
100 g (3½ oz) chestnut
  mushrooms, chopped
100 g (3½ oz) shiitake
  mushrooms, sliced
250 g (8 oz) pearl barley
1.5 litres (2½ pints) mushroom
  or vegetable stock
1 tablespoon white miso paste
small handful of thyme sprigs,
  leaves picked, plus extra
  leaves to garnish
100 g (3½ oz) crème fraîche
100 g (3½ oz) vegetarian Italian
  hard cheese, finely grated,
  plus extra to serve
salt and pepper

*For the garlic mushrooms*
1 tablespoon olive oil
75 g (3 oz) shiitake mushrooms,
  sliced
3 garlic cloves, crushed
1 tablespoon unsalted butter

Heat the oil in a large frying pan, add the onion and leek and fry over a medium-low heat for about 5 minutes until soft and the onion is translucent. Stir in the garlic and fry for a few minutes until softened. Add the mushrooms and fry for a further 3–4 minutes until just tender and beginning to turn golden.

Transfer the mushroom mixture to the slow cooker and add the pearl barley, stock, miso paste and thyme. Cover with the lid and cook on high for 2½ hours until the barley is tender and the sauce thickened. Stir through the crème fraîche and cheese and season to taste with salt and pepper.

Cook the garlic-fried mushrooms 10 minutes before the end of the risotto cooking time. Heat the oil in a large frying pan and add the sliced mushrooms. Fry over a medium-low heat for 3 minutes until beginning to soften. Add the crushed garlic and continue to fry for 2 minutes until the mushrooms are golden brown. Add the butter to the pan and toss to coat the mushrooms. Season with salt and pepper.

Spoon the risotto into serving bowls, then sprinkle with thyme leaves and drizzle with good-quality olive oil. Serve with extra grated cheese and the garlic-fried mushrooms.

**SERVES 4–6**
Preparation time 1 hour
Cooking time 2½ hours

# POTATO, FENNEL & CELERIAC BAKE

1 celeriac, about 500 g
   (1 lb), peeled
500 g (1 lb) floury potatoes
   (such as Maris Piper), peeled
1 fennel bulb, trimmed
50 g (2 oz) butter, plus extra
   for greasing
4 garlic cloves, finely chopped
50 g (2 oz) plain flour
1 litre (1¾ pints) milk
50 g (2 oz) Emmental
   cheese, grated
good grating of nutmeg
50 g (2 oz) walnuts
50 g (2 oz) fresh breadcrumbs
2 tablespoons olive oil
50 g (2 oz) vegetarian Italian
   hard cheese, grated
salt and pepper
steamed greens or a nut roast
   or whole baked cauliflower,
   to serve

Slice the vegetables as thinly as possible. Grease the slow cooker pot well with butter, then layer the vegetables in the pot so they are well mixed, scattering the garlic between the layers as you go.

Melt the butter in a saucepan over a medium heat, then add the flour and stir together until it resembles a sandy-coloured paste. Cook for a few minutes until it begins to smell biscuity, then pour in a small amount of the milk, remove the pan from the heat and whisk vigorously until smooth. Return the pan to the heat and continue to add the milk in small amounts, whisking until smooth after each addition, until all the milk has been added. Simmer for about 5 minutes until the sauce is smooth and thick. Add the Emmental and nutmeg, then season with salt and pepper. Continue to cook for a few minutes, stirring continuously, until the sauce is smooth.

Pour the sauce over the vegetables in the slow cooker, ensuring they are evenly covered. Cover with the lid and cook on high for 2 hours until the sauce is thickened and the vegetables are tender.

Meanwhile, put the walnuts into a food processor and pulse until they resemble fine crumbs. Tip into a bowl, add the breadcrumbs and oil and season well. Mix together until combined, then set aside.

Preheat the oven to 180°C (350°F), Gas Mark 4. Carefully transfer the vegetables to an ovenproof dish. Sprinkle the walnut breadcrumbs and grated cheese evenly over the top, then transfer to the oven and cook for 30 minutes until golden brown and the cheese is melted and bubbling. Leave to stand for 5–10 minutes. Serve with steamed greens, or with a nut roast or whole baked cauliflower.

SERVES 4
**Preparation time 15 minutes**
**Cooking time 3 hours**

# MAC & CHEESE WITH LEEKS & CRISPY BREADCRUMB TOPPING

50 g (2 oz) cream cheese

500 ml (17 fl oz) milk

25 g (1 oz) butter, melted

100 g (3½ oz) Cheddar cheese, grated

100 g (3½ oz) Emmental cheese, grated

50 g (2 oz) vegetarian Italian hard cheese, grated

1 tablespoon wholegrain mustard

½ teaspoon cayenne pepper

2 garlic cloves, crushed

250 g (8 oz) dried macaroni (curved elbow macaroni, if possible)

1 leek, trimmed, cleaned and finely chopped

salt and pepper

1 tablespoon finely chopped chives, to garnish

*For the topping*

25 g (1 oz) fresh or dried panko breadcrumbs

25 g (1 oz) Emmental cheese, grated

Whisk together the cream cheese and milk in a small jug until smooth. Pour into the slow cooker, then add the melted butter, cheeses, mustard, cayenne pepper and garlic and mix together. Stir in the dried pasta and chopped leek and mix until they are well coated in the sauce.

Cover with the lid and cook on low for 2½ hours until the pasta is tender and the sauce is thick and creamy. Season to taste with salt and plenty of pepper and spoon into a 16 x 22 cm (6¼ x 8½ inch) ovenproof dish.

If making this the day before, leave to cool and then place in the refrigerator overnight. When you're ready to eat, preheat the oven to 180°C (350°F), Gas Mark 4. Remove the dish from the refrigerator, cover with foil and place in the oven for 20 minutes until warmed through. Remove the foil.

Preheat the grill. Sprinkle over the breadcrumbs and grated cheese. Place under the grill for 3 minutes until golden and the cheese has melted.

Serve immediately, sprinkled with the chives.

**SERVES 4**
Preparation time 20 minutes
Cooking time 2½–3 hours

# MUSHROOM & TOMATO RIGATONI

250 g (8 oz) rigatoni or
    pasta quills
3 tablespoons olive oil
1 onion, sliced
2–3 garlic cloves, finely chopped
250 g (8 oz) closed cup
    mushrooms, sliced
250 g (8 oz) portobello
    mushrooms, sliced
250 g (8 oz) tomatoes, cut
    into chunks
400 g (13 oz) can chopped
    tomatoes
200 ml (7 fl oz) vegetable stock
    or dry white wine
1 tablespoon tomato purée
3 rosemary sprigs
salt and pepper
freshly grated vegetarian Italian
    hard cheese, to garnish
rocket salad, to serve

Put the pasta into a large bowl, cover with boiling water and leave to stand for 10 minutes while preparing the rest of the dish.

Heat 1 tablespoon of the oil in a large frying pan, add the onion and fry until softened. Stir in the remaining oil, garlic and mushrooms and fry, stirring, until the mushrooms are just beginning to brown.

Stir in the fresh and canned tomatoes, stock or wine and tomato purée. Add the rosemary and a little salt and pepper and bring to the boil.

Drain the pasta and put it in the slow cooker pot, pour over the hot mushroom mixture and spread into an even layer. Cover with the lid and cook on low for 2½–3 hours or until the pasta is just tender. Spoon into shallow bowls and sprinkle with grated cheese. Serve with a rocket salad.

**SERVES 6**
Preparation time 50 minutes
Cooking time 2½ hours

# LEMONY GREENS & FETA FILO PIE

500 g (1 lb) Swiss chard, sliced
200 g (7 oz) cavolo nero, stems
   removed and leaves shredded
3 garlic cloves, finely chopped
grated zest and juice of
   1 unwaxed lemon
100 ml (3½ fl oz) vegetable
   stock
3 eggs, beaten
good grating of nutmeg
250 g (8 oz) feta cheese,
   crumbled
20 g (¾ oz) parsley, chopped
small handful of mint
   leaves, chopped
270 g (9 oz) packet filo
   pastry sheets
100 g (3½ oz) butter, melted
1 tablespoon sesame seeds
salt and pepper
green salad leaves, to serve

Put the chard, cavolo nero, garlic, lemon juice and stock into the slow cooker. Season well with salt and pepper and stir. Cover with the lid and cook on high for 2 hours until the vegetables are tender.

Line a sieve with kitchen paper, then tip the cooked greens into the sieve and drain, using more kitchen paper to squeeze out as much liquid as possible. Transfer to a large bowl and leave to cool, then add the eggs, a good grating of nutmeg, the feta, chopped herbs and lemon zest and mix together. Set aside.

Preheat the oven to 200°C (400°F), Gas Mark 6. Reserve 2 filo sheets for the top of the pie. Brush 1 of the remaining sheets of filo pastry with melted butter, then place in a 20 cm (8 inch) springform or round cake tin to cover half the bottom of the tin and up the sides, leaving a generous amount of overhanging pastry. Repeat with more layers of buttered filo, working your way around the tin until the bottom and sides are covered.

Tip the chard mixture into the filo case and smooth the surface, then fold the overhanging sheets of filo over the top to enclose the filling. Brush the reserved filo sheets with butter, then scrunch up and place on top. Sprinkle with the sesame seeds. Place the tin on a baking sheet and bake in the middle of the oven for 30 minutes until crisp and golden brown.

Leave to cool in the tin for about 10 minutes, then carefully remove the pie from the tin and slide on to a plate. Serve with a fresh green salad. It's great with buttery new potatoes too.

SERVES 6
**Preparation time 55 minutes**
**Cooking time 2 hours**

# BEETROOT RISOTTO WITH STILTON & WALNUTS

400 g (13 oz) fresh beetroot,
   peeled and chopped into
   3 cm (1¼ inch) cubes
2 tablespoons olive oil
1 teaspoon fennel seeds
100 ml (3½ fl oz) water
1 onion, finely chopped
2 garlic cloves, crushed
250 g (8 oz) arborio rice
200 ml (7 fl oz) red wine
1 litre (1¾ pints) vegetable stock
100 g (3½ oz) walnuts
50 g (2 oz) butter
100 g (3½ oz) Stilton or
   other hard blue cheese,
   rind removed
salt and pepper
small handful of dill fronds,
   to garnish

Preheat the oven to 180°C (350°F), Gas Mark 4. Put the beetroot on a baking tray. Drizzle with 1 tablespoon of the oil, sprinkle with the fennel seeds and season with salt and pepper. Toss until coated. Roast for 40 minutes until tender. Leave to cool slightly, then tip two-thirds of the beetroot into a food processor or blender, pour in the measured water and blitz to a purée. Set aside the remaining beetroot.

Meanwhile, heat the remaining oil in a frying pan, add the onion and fry over a medium-low heat for 5 minutes until soft and translucent, then stir in the garlic and fry for a few minutes until softened. Add the rice and cook for a further few minutes, stirring until well coated in the onion mixture and the rice makes a light popping sound. Pour in the wine and bring to the boil, then bubble until reduced by half.

Transfer the rice mixture to the slow cooker, add the beetroot purée and stock and season well. Cover with the lid and cook on low for 2 hours until the rice is tender and the sauce thickened and glossy.

Meanwhile, heat a large, dry frying pan over a medium-low heat, add the walnuts and toast for 5 minutes, stirring frequently, until golden brown. Leave to cool, then roughly chop. Set aside.

When the risotto is cooked, add the butter and stir through until melted, then stir in the reserved beetroot. Adjust the seasoning to taste. Spoon into bowls, crumble over the blue cheese and top with the toasted walnuts. Serve sprinkled with the dill fronds.

SERVES 4
Preparation time 20 minutes
Cooking time 2¾–3 hours 20 minutes

# AUBERGINES WITH BAKED EGGS

4 tablespoons olive oil

1 onion, chopped

2 medium aubergines, cubed

2 garlic cloves, finely chopped

500 g (1 lb) tomatoes, cut into
   large chunks

½ teaspoon smoked paprika,
   plus extra (optional)
   to garnish

½ teaspoon ground cumin

½ teaspoon ground coriander

100 g (3½ oz) quinoa

300 ml (½ pint) vegetable stock

125 g (4 oz) frozen peas
   (optional)

4 eggs

salt and pepper

chopped mint, to garnish

toasted pitta breads, cut into
   strips, to serve

Heat the oil in a large frying pan, add the onion and aubergines and fry, stirring, until the aubergines are golden.

Stir in the garlic, tomatoes and spices and cook for 1 minute. Mix in the quinoa and stock, add a little salt and pepper and bring to the boil. Transfer the mixture to the slow cooker pot. Cover with the lid and cook on high for 2½–3 hours.

Stir in the frozen peas, if using, and add a little boiling water if the quinoa has begun to stick around the edges of the pot. Make 4 dips with a spoon, then break and drop an egg into each dip. Cover and cook for 15–20 minutes or until the egg whites are set and the yolks still soft.

Spoon on to plates, sprinkle the eggs with a little extra salt and pepper or some more smoked paprika and garnish with chopped mint. Serve with toasted pitta breads, cut into strips.

SERVES 4
**Preparation time 30 minutes**
**Cooking time 1 hour 40 minutes**

# CREAMY ORZO WITH GREEN VEG

50 g (2 oz) butter, plus extra
   to serve
2 tablespoons olive oil
1 onion, finely chopped
3 garlic cloves, crushed
150 g (5 oz) orzo pasta
200 ml (7 fl oz) white wine
500 ml (17 fl oz) vegetable stock
150 g (5 oz) frozen broad beans
100 g (3½ oz) cavolo nero, stems
   removed and leaves shredded
1 courgette, finely chopped
100 g (3½ oz) vegetarian Italian
   hard cheese, grated, plus
   extra to serve
salt and pepper
handful of basil leaves,
   to garnish

Heat the butter and oil in a large frying pan until melted and frothy. Add the onion and a pinch of salt and cook over a medium-low heat for 5 minutes until soft and translucent, then stir in the garlic and fry for a few minutes until softened. Add the orzo and cook for a further few minutes, stirring until well coated in the onion mixture and it begins to sizzle. Pour in the wine and bring to the boil, then bubble until reduced by half.

Transfer the orzo mixture to the slow cooker and pour in the stock, stirring until combined. Cover with the lid and cook on high for 1½ hours.

Stir in the frozen broad beans, cavolo nero and courgette, replace the lid and cook, still on high, for a further 10 minutes until the vegetables are tender.

Add the cheese and a knob of butter to the cooked orzo, then stir through until melted and silky. Season to taste with salt and pepper.

When ready to serve, stack the basil leaves in a pile, then roll up and thinly slice into ribbons. Serve immediately, sprinkled with the basil and a good grating of cheese.

**SERVES 4**
**Preparation time 35 minutes**
**Cooking time 3 hours**

# VEGETARIAN SAUSAGE & WHITE BEAN STEW

3 tablespoons olive oil

1 onion, chopped

2 garlic cloves, sliced

8 vegetarian sausages

2 carrots, thickly sliced

1 leek, trimmed, cleaned and
   thickly sliced

400 g (13 oz) can chopped
   tomatoes

200 ml (7 fl oz) red wine

2 tablespoons tomato purée

2 roasted red peppers from a
   jar, thinly sliced

pinch of dried chilli flakes

½ teaspoon dried oregano

2 rosemary sprigs

2 thyme sprigs

400 g (13 oz) can haricot or
   cannellini beans, drained
   and rinsed

100 g (3½ oz) kale, stems
   removed and leaves
   roughly torn

salt and pepper

2 tablespoons chopped parsley,
   to garnish

mashed potato, to serve

Heat 2 tablespoons of the oil in a large frying pan, add the onion and
fry over a medium-low heat for 5 minutes until soft and translucent.
Stir in the garlic and fry for 3 minutes until the onion and garlic are
lightly golden. Transfer to the slow cooker.

Return the pan to the heat, add the remaining oil and the vegetarian
sausages and fry for about 15 minutes until golden brown on all sides.

Transfer the sausages to the slow cooker and add the carrots, leek,
chopped tomatoes, wine, tomato purée, red peppers, chilli flakes and
oregano. Fill up the chopped tomatoes can with water, right to the top,
then pour in. Season well with salt and pepper, then add the rosemary
and thyme. Cover with the lid and cook on high for 2 hours.

Stir in the beans, replace the lid and cook for a further 50 minutes, then
add the kale. Replace the lid and continue to cook for 10 minutes until
the kale is tender. Adjust the seasoning to taste.

Garnish the stew with the chopped parsley and serve with creamy
mashed potato.

**SERVES 4**
**Preparation time 20 minutes**
**Cooking time 2 hours**

# COCONUT DHAL WITH PANEER

1 tablespoon coconut oil

1 onion, chopped

3 garlic cloves, finely chopped

1 thumb-sized piece of fresh
   root ginger, peeled and
   finely chopped

1 red chilli, deseeded and
   finely chopped

1 teaspoon ground cumin

1 teaspoon mustard seeds

2 teaspoons ground turmeric

1 teaspoon curry powder

350 g (11½ oz) red lentils

400 ml (14 fl oz) can coconut
   milk

600 ml (1 pint) vegetable stock

150 g (5 oz) fresh spinach leaves

small handful of fresh
   coriander, chopped

salt and pepper

*For the toppings*

1 tablespoon groundnut oil,
   plus extra if necessary

200 g (7 oz) paneer, cut into
   bite-sized cubes

10 curry leaves

1 tablespoon mustard seeds

*To serve*

warm roti

mango chutney

yogurt (optional)

Heat the coconut oil in a large frying pan, add the onion and fry over a medium-low heat for 5 minutes until soft and translucent, then stir in the garlic, ginger, chilli and dried spices and fry for a few minutes until fragrant.

Transfer the onion mixture to the slow cooker, add the lentils, coconut milk and stock and season with salt and pepper, then stir well until combined. Cook on high for 2 hours until the lentils are tender and soft, and the sauce is thick and creamy.

Turn off the slow cooker, then stir in the spinach and coriander. Replace the lid and leave to wilt in the residual heat.

Meanwhile, heat the groundnut oil in a frying pan, add the paneer cubes and cook over a medium-high heat for about 1 minute on each side until golden brown, carefully turning the pieces to ensure they are golden on all sides. Remove from the pan with a slotted spoon and drain on kitchen paper.

Add a little more groundnut oil to the pan, if needed, then add the curry leaves and mustard seeds and fry for 1–2 minutes until the seeds begin to pop.

Spoon the dhal into serving bowls, then top with the crispy paneer cubes and a drizzle of the spice-infused oil, with the curry leaves and mustard seeds. Serve with warm roti and mango chutney, and dollops of yogurt, if liked.

SERVES 4–6
Preparation time 15 minutes
Cooking time 3 hours 10 minutes

# BUTTERNUT SQUASH, CARROT & FENNEL SOUP

1 butternut squash, peeled, deseeded and chopped, about 500 g (1 lb) prepared weight
650 g (1 lb 7 oz) carrots, roughly chopped
1 fennel bulb, trimmed and sliced
1 litre (1¾ pints) vegetable stock
1 teaspoon curry powder
½ teaspoon ground cumin
½ teaspoon ground cinnamon
½ teaspoon fennel seeds
½ teaspoon dried chilli flakes

*For the crunchy seed topping (optional)*
50 g (2 oz) pumpkin seeds
50 g (2 oz) sunflower seeds
50 g (2 oz) linseeds
1 tablespoon poppy seeds
1 tablespoon olive oil
½ teaspoon smoked paprika
½ teaspoon garlic granules
½ teaspoon dried rosemary

Put all the soup ingredients into the slow cooker, cover with the lid and cook on high for 3 hours until the vegetables are tender and cooked through.

Meanwhile, make the seed topping, if using. Preheat the oven to 180°C (350°F), Gas Mark 4. Mix together all the ingredients in a bowl until the seeds are well coated in the oil, then spread evenly on a baking sheet lined with greaseproof paper. Place in the oven for about 10 minutes until golden. Remove and leave to cool. Keep to one side what you want to use for the soup and store any remaining seed topping in an airtight container in a cool, dark place for up to 4 weeks.

Turn off the slow cooker and leave the soup to cool slightly, then purée while still in the slow cooker pot using a stick blender. Alternatively, carefully transfer the soup to a blender and blend, in batches if necessary, until smooth, then return to the slow cooker.

Season to taste with salt and pepper. Cook the soup on high for a further 10 minutes, to warm through.

Ladle into bowls and serve topped with a sprinkling of the crunchy seeds, if liked. You could add a little chopped parsley as well for a splash of vibrant colour.

SERVES 4
**Preparation time** 10 minutes
**Cooking time** 3 hours

# SWEET POTATO CURRY WITH TOASTED CASHEWS

200 g (7 oz) red lentils, rinsed
1 onion, chopped
2 garlic cloves, crushed
1 thumb-sized piece of fresh
    root ginger, peeled and grated
3 sweet potatoes, peeled
    and cubed
2 tablespoons vegetarian
    red Thai curry paste
1 teaspoon garam masala
1 teaspoon ground turmeric
2 makrut lime leaves
2 tablespoons tomato purée
500 ml (17 fl oz) vegetable stock
400 ml (14 fl oz) can coconut
    milk
100 g (3½ oz) cashew nuts
salt and pepper

*To serve*
1 red chilli, deseeded and
    finely sliced
handful of fresh coriander,
    chopped
brown or wild rice

Put all the ingredients, except the cashews, into the slow cooker and stir together until the tomato purée is incorporated and the sauce well combined. Cover with the lid and cook on high for 3 hours until the lentils and sweet potatoes are tender and the sauce is thick.

When almost ready to serve, heat a large, dry frying pan over a medium-low heat, add the cashews and toast for about 5 minutes, stirring frequently, until golden brown. Alternatively, put on a baking tray and roast in an oven preheated to 180°C (350°F), Gas Mark 4, for 2 minutes. Remove the tray from the oven and carefully shake to mix the cashews. Return to the oven for about 3 minutes until the cashews are golden brown. Leave to cool slightly, then roughly chop.

Season the curry to taste with salt and pepper, then spoon into serving bowls and sprinkle with the toasted cashews, sliced chilli and chopped coriander. Serve with brown or wild rice.

SERVES 4
**Preparation time 25 minutes**
**Cooking time 2 hours 20 minutes**

# SAG ALOO WITH PANEER

1 tablespoon coconut oil

1 onion, chopped

4 garlic cloves, chopped

5 cm (2 inch) piece of fresh root ginger, peeled and chopped

1 tablespoon garam masala

1 tablespoon ground turmeric

1 tablespoon ground cumin

1 tablespoon ground coriander

1 teaspoon mustard seeds

1 green chilli, deseeded and finely chopped

875 g (1¾ lb) frozen spinach, defrosted, drained and chopped

100 g (3½ oz) baby new potatoes, chopped into bite-sized cubes

200 g (7 oz) passata (sieved tomatoes)

400 ml (14 fl oz) can coconut milk

200 g (7 oz) fresh spinach leaves, finely chopped

200 g (7 oz) paneer, cut into bite-sized cubes

salt

steamed basmati rice or warm roti, to serve

Heat the coconut oil in a frying pan, add the onion and fry over a medium-low heat for 5 minutes until soft and translucent, then stir in the garlic, ginger, dried spices and green chilli and fry for a few minutes until fragrant.

Transfer the onion mixture to the slow cooker, add the defrosted spinach, potatoes, passata and coconut milk and season well with salt. Mix together, then cover with the lid and cook on high for 2 hours.

Stir in the fresh spinach and paneer cubes, replace the lid and cook, still on high, for a further 20 minutes until the sauce has reduced and thickened.

Serve with steamed basmati rice, or warm roti if you prefer, or as a side dish with other curries.

SERVES 4
**Preparation time 15 minutes**
**Cooking time 2 hours**

# HOISIN PULLED JACKFRUIT

1 tablespoon sesame oil

2 garlic cloves, crushed

3 cm (1¼ inch) piece of fresh
   root ginger, peeled and grated

2 x 400 g (13 oz) cans jackfruit,
   drained

1 teaspoon Chinese five spice

2 tablespoons soy sauce

3 tablespoons hoisin sauce, plus
   extra for brushing and serving

1 teaspoon mirin

*To serve*

8 Chinese pancakes

½ cucumber, cut into long,
   thin strips

handful of spring onions, cut
   into long, thin strips

black and white sesame seeds

Heat the sesame oil in a frying pan, and add the garlic and ginger. Fry over a medium-low heat for a few minutes until softened and fragrant.

Transfer the mixture to the slow cooker, add the jackfruit, five spice, soy sauce, hoisin sauce and mirin and mix together. Cover with the lid and cook on high for 2 hours.

Preheat the grill. Carefully remove the jackfruit from the slow cooker and spread out on a baking tray. Brush with more hoisin sauce, then place under the grill for 5 minutes until caramelized and browned on the edges.

Serve with Chinese pancakes, strips of cucumber and spring onions, some extra hoisin sauce and a sprinkle of sesame seeds.

SERVES 4
**Preparation time 15 minutes**
**Cooking time 1 hour 40 minutes**

# KIMCHI NOODLE SOUP

**4 spring onions, finely sliced,
plus extra to serve**

**4 garlic cloves, finely chopped**

**20 g (¾ oz) fresh root ginger,
peeled and cut into
fine matchsticks**

**50 g (2 oz) dried shiitake
mushrooms**

**4 tablespoons light soy sauce,
or more to taste**

**1.5 litres (2½ pints) boiling
water**

**100 g (3½ oz) kimchi, drained**

**200 g (7 oz) dried ramen noodles
or buckwheat soba noodles**

**2 tablespoons lime juice**

Put the spring onions, garlic, ginger, dried mushrooms, soy sauce and measured boiling water into the slow cooker, cover with the lid and cook on high for 1½ hours.

Stir in the kimchi and noodles, replace the lid and cook, still on high, for a further 5–10 minutes until the noodles are tender.

Season the soup with the lime juice and more soy sauce if needed. Serve immediately, topped with extra finely sliced spring onions.

**SERVES 2**
Preparation time 20 minutes
Cooking time 1½ hours

# MIXED MUSHROOM STROGANOFF

2 tablespoons vegetable oil
6 large portobello or flat
   mushrooms, sliced
1 large onion, thinly sliced
2 garlic cloves, thinly sliced
1 tablespoon sweet
   smoked paprika
1 tablespoon tomato purée
1 tablespoon Dijon mustard
20 g (¾ oz) dried porcini
   mushrooms, crumbled
150 ml (¼ pint) hot vegan
   bouillon stock
150 ml (¼ pint) dairy-free
   soured cream
1 teaspoon apple cider vinegar,
   or more to taste
salt and pepper

*To serve*
warm bread (optional)
rice or pasta (optional)
small handful of flat leaf
   parsley, chopped

Heat the oil in a large frying pan over a high heat, add the mushrooms and sauté for about 3 minutes on each side until golden brown. Transfer to the slow cooker.

Add the onion to the frying pan and sauté for 5 minutes until beginning to soften and colour, adding the garlic for the last minute of the cooking time.

Transfer the onion and garlic mixture to the slow cooker and add all the remaining ingredients, seasoning well with salt and pepper.

Cover with the lid and cook on high for 1½ hours until the sauce has thickened and looks creamy.

Check and adjust the seasoning, adding a dash more vinegar if needed, and serve immediately with some warm bread or over rice or pasta, sprinkled with the chopped parsley.

**SERVES 4**
Preparation time 20 minutes
Cooking time 1½ hours

# GREEN BEAN CURRY

2 tablespoons coconut oil, plus
   1 tablespoon for the curry leaf
   garnish (optional)
2 tablespoons mustard seeds
10 fresh curry leaves, plus extra
   to garnish (optional)
1 tablespoon mild curry powder
1 teaspoon ground turmeric
¼ teaspoon ground cloves
1 large red onion, finely sliced
3 garlic cloves, finely sliced
500 g (1 lb) runner beans,
   trimmed, strings removed and
   cut on the diagonal into 2 cm
   (¾ inch) pieces
400 ml (14 fl oz) can coconut
   milk
2 large tomatoes, roughly
   chopped, or ½ x 400 g (13 oz)
   can chopped tomatoes
finely grated zest and juice of
   1 unwaxed lime, plus extra
   lime wedges, to serve
salt (optional)
rice or flatbreads, to serve

Heat the coconut oil in a small frying pan over a medium heat, add the mustard seeds and curry leaves and cook until the seeds begin to pop. Stir in the rest of the spices and cook for 1 minute.

Transfer the spice mixture to the slow cooker, add the onion, garlic and beans and toss to coat. Stir in the coconut milk and tomatoes. Fill the coconut milk can with water and add to the slow cooker, then cover with the lid and cook on high for 1½ hours.

Season with the lime zest and juice, and salt if needed. If using curry leaves to garnish, fry in 1 tablespoon coconut oil until they have crisped up, then scatter over the finished dish. Serve immediately with lime wedges and rice or flatbreads.

**SERVES 4**
Preparation time 30 minutes
Cooking time 2–2½ hours

# MOROCCAN MEATLESS MEATBALLS

1 shallot, quartered

1 garlic clove, peeled

15 g (½ oz) fresh root ginger, peeled

1 red chilli

large handful of fresh coriander, plus extra, chopped, to garnish

1 preserved lemon

400 g (13 oz) meat-free mince

1 slice of stale white bread, torn

½ tablespoon ground cumin

½ tablespoon ground coriander

1 teaspoon ground cinnamon

1 tablespoon Dijon mustard

1 tablespoon tomato purée

2 teaspoons pomegranate molasses

1 tablespoon olive oil (optional)

couscous with fruit and nuts, to serve (optional)

*For the sauce*

1 red onion, finely chopped

2 garlic cloves, finely chopped

400 g (13 oz) can chopped tomatoes

1 tablespoon tomato purée

150 ml (¼ pint) hot vegan bouillon stock

1 tablespoon pomegranate molasses

1 tablespoon ras el hanout

1 tablespoon ground cumin

salt and pepper

Put all the sauce ingredients into the slow cooker, cover with the lid and cook on high for 1 hour.

Meanwhile, put the shallot, garlic, ginger, chilli and coriander, stalks and all, in a food processor. Halve the preserved lemon, scrape out the flesh with a teaspoon and discard it, finely chop the rind and add to the food processor. Blitz until you have a slightly chunky paste. Add the remaining ingredients, except the oil, season well with salt and pepper and pulse to combine. To make sure the mixture is fully combined, squeeze it together with your hands.

Preheat the oven to 200°C (400°F), Gas Mark 6. Divide the meatball mixture into even pieces, roll each into a small golf ball-sized ball and place on a baking tray lined with nonstick baking paper. Toss the meatballs in the oil to coat and roast in the oven for 15–20 minutes until browned and caramelized. Alternatively, you can skip this step and simply poach the meatballs in the sauce.

Stir the roasted or unroasted meatballs gently into the sauce, replace the lid and cook, still on high, for a further 1–1½ hours until the sauce has reduced and thickened and the meatballs are cooked through.

Serve immediately, being careful when handling the meatballs as they will be quite delicate. Sprinkle with the freshly chopped coriander, along with couscous tossed with dried cranberries or raisins and pine nuts or flaked almonds, if you like.

SERVES 4–6
Preparation time 20 minutes
Cooking time 2 hours 10 minutes–2 hours 40 minutes

# SWEET POTATO MAC & CHEESE

3 large sweet potatoes
  (about 500 g/1 lb), peeled
  and cut into 3–4 cm
  (1¼–1½ inch) chunks
1 shallot, sliced
2 garlic cloves, sliced
100 g (3½ oz) cashew nuts
5 tablespoons nutritional yeast
1 tablespoon Dijon mustard
300 ml (½ pint) unsweetened
  almond milk
300 ml (½ pint) hot vegan
  bouillon stock
¼ teaspoon freshly grated
  nutmeg
350 g (11½ oz) dried macaroni
1½ tablespoons apple
  cider vinegar
2 tablespoons vegetable or
  sunflower oil
100 g (3½ oz) panko
  breadcrumbs
3 thyme sprigs, leaves picked
salt and pepper
leafy salad, to serve (optional)

Put the sweet potatoes, shallot, garlic, cashews, nutritional yeast, mustard, almond milk, hot stock, nutmeg and a good grinding of pepper into the slow cooker. Cover with the lid and cook on high for 2–2½ hours until the sweet potato is easily pierced with a fork.

Meanwhile, cook the macaroni in a large saucepan of salted boiling water according to the packet instructions until firm to the bite. Drain, rinse under cold running water until cool and leave to drain.

Use an immersion blender to blend the sweet potato mixture until smooth and creamy, then season to taste with salt and the vinegar. Stir in the cooked macaroni, replace the lid and cook, still on high, for a further 10 minutes until the pasta is warmed through.

To make the breadcrumb topping, heat the oil in a wide-based pan over a medium heat. Add the breadcrumbs and cook, stirring frequently until golden brown.

When the pasta is warmed through, serve immediately, garnished with the toasted breadcrumbs and thyme leaves, with a lightly dressed leafy salad on the side, if you like.

**SERVES 2**
Preparation time 25 minutes
Cooking time 1 hour 10 minutes

# BUTTER BEANS WITH FENNEL, CAPERS & OLIVES

..............................................................................................................................................

3 tablespoons olive oil

2 shallots, finely sliced

1 large fennel bulb, finely sliced

2 garlic cloves, finely sliced

400 g (13 oz) can butter beans,
   drained and rinsed

350 ml (12 fl oz) hot vegan
   bouillon stock

100 g (3½ oz) pitted Spanish
   Gordal olives, halved

100 g (3½ oz) capers in
   brine, drained

finely grated zest and juice of
   1 unwaxed lemon

salt and pepper

very large handful of flat leaf
   parsley, roughly chopped,
   to serve

Heat the oil in a frying pan over a medium-low heat, add the shallots and fennel and sauté for about 10 minutes until beginning to soften and colour. Add the garlic and sauté for a further 1–2 minutes.

Transfer the shallot mixture to the slow cooker and add the butter beans and hot stock. Cover with the lid and cook on high for 1 hour.

Stir in the olives and capers, replace the lid and cook, still on high, for a further 5–10 minutes until warmed through.

Add the lemon zest and juice, season to taste with salt and pepper and serve immediately, sprinkled with the parsley.

**SERVES 4**
Preparation time 15 minutes
Cooking time 2½ hours

# KUNG PAO CAULIFLOWER

1 large cauliflower, broken
   into florets
1 red pepper, cored, deseeded
   and thickly sliced
2 garlic cloves, grated
15 g (½ oz) fresh root ginger,
   peeled and grated
4 spring onions, thinly sliced,
   white and green parts
   kept separate
½ teaspoon dried chilli flakes
50 ml (2 fl oz) soy sauce
50 ml (2 fl oz) hot vegan
   bouillon stock
2 tablespoons hoisin sauce
2 tablespoons maple syrup
2 tablespoons rice vinegar
1 tablespoon sesame oil, plus
   extra for drizzling
1 tablespoon cornflour

*To serve*
50 g (2 oz) roasted, salted
   peanuts, roughly chopped
small handful of fresh
   coriander leaves
1 lime, cut into wedges

Put all the ingredients, except the cornflour, into the slow cooker and toss until well combined. Cover with the lid and cook on high for 2 hours.

Remove 2 tablespoons of the cooking liquid and mix with the cornflour in a cup until smooth. Stir the cornflour mixture into the cauliflower mixture, replace the lid and cook, still on high, for a further 30 minutes until the sauce has thickened.

Serve immediately, sprinkled with the chopped peanuts and coriander leaves and the lime wedges alongside.

**SERVES 4**
Preparation time 25 minutes
Cooking time 1–1½ hours

# CORN CHOWDER

2 tablespoons olive oil
1 large onion, finely sliced, or
 1 leek, trimmed, cleaned and
 finely sliced
2 garlic cloves, finely sliced
2 large floury potatoes,
 peeled and cut into 1 cm
 (½ inch) cubes
500 ml (17 fl oz) hot vegan
 bouillon stock
2 thyme sprigs, leaves picked
3 corn on the cob, kernels sliced
 from the cob, cobs reserved
 and a large handful of kernels
 reserved to garnish
juice of 1 unwaxed lemon, zest
 reserved to garnish
salt and pepper

*To garnish*
2 red chillies, finely chopped
handful of chives,
 finely chopped

Heat the oil in a frying pan over a medium heat, add the onion or leek and sauté for about 10 minutes until softened. Add the garlic and cook for a further minute.

Transfer the onion or leek and garlic to the slow cooker and add the potatoes, hot stock, thyme leaves and corn kernels, along with the cobs for extra corn flavour. Cover with the lid and cook on high for 1–1½ hours until the potatoes are easily pierced with a fork. Season with the lemon juice and salt and pepper to taste.

Remove the cobs and serve immediately, sprinkled with the reserved corn kernels, charred in a pan, the reserved lemon zest and the finely chopped chilli and chives.

**SERVES 4–6**
Preparation time 30–45 minutes
Cooking time 2–2½ hours

# SQUASH MOUSSAKA

*For the moussaka*
3 tablespoons extra virgin
   olive oil
1 large butternut squash,
   peeled, deseeded and
   very thinly sliced
400 g (13 oz) meat-free mince
1 red onion, finely chopped
1 garlic clove, finely chopped
400 g (13 oz) can plum tomatoes
1 tablespoon vegan bouillon
   stock powder
1 teaspoon dried oregano
½ teaspoon dried mint
1 teaspoon ground cinnamon
1 tablespoon tomato purée
2 teaspoons Marmite
salt and pepper
green salad, to serve

*For the béchamel sauce*
2 tablespoons vegetable oil
3 tablespoons cornflour
400 ml (14 fl oz) soya or
   unsweetened almond milk
1 bay leaf
½ teaspoon onion powder
¼ teaspoon freshly grated
   nutmeg
2 tablespoons nutritional yeast

Grease the slow cooker pot with 1 tablespoon of the oil. Cover the bottom with a thin layer of squash slices, reserving the remainder.

Heat the remaining 2 tablespoons of oil in a large frying pan over a medium heat, add the meat-free mince and cook until golden brown. Add the onion and cook for 5 minutes until soft and translucent. Stir in the garlic and cook for a further minute. Add the tomatoes and break them up with a wooden spoon. Swill the tomato can out with water and pour in. Add the stock powder to the can, fill with boiling water, stir and pour in. Add the dried herbs, cinnamon, tomato purée, Marmite and plenty of seasoning and bring to the boil.

Spread a layer of this mixture over the squash. Repeat with 2 or 3 more alternating layers. Cover with the lid and cook on high for 1 hour.

Meanwhile, heat the vegetable oil in a small saucepan over a medium heat, add the cornflour and whisk for 1 minute until you have a smooth paste. Gradually add the dairy-free milk, whisking well after each addition. Add the remaining ingredients, bring to the boil, whisking constantly, and cook for about 10 minutes until thick and smooth. Remove the bay leaf, season and set aside. If your sauce is lumpy, blitz it in a blender or pass it through a sieve.

Spread the sauce evenly over the top of the moussaka, replace the lid, positioned slightly ajar, and cook, still on high, for another 1–1½ hours until the squash is easily pierced with a fork and the béchamel looks dry on top. Serve immediately with a simple green salad.

**SERVES 6**
Preparation time 20 minutes
Cooking time 1 hour

# KATSU CURRY SAUCE

2 carrots, peeled and
    finely chopped
2 onions, finely chopped
4 garlic cloves, finely chopped
20 g (¾ oz) fresh root ginger,
    peeled and finely grated
2 tablespoons plain flour
400 ml (14 fl oz) hot vegan
    bouillon stock
2 tablespoons garam masala
1 tablespoon curry powder
1 tablespoon maple syrup
1 tablespoon soy sauce
juice of 1 lime
1 teaspoon sea salt
1 bay leaf

*To serve*
breadcrumbed seitan or tofu
fresh salad
sesame seeds
white rice
1 lime, cut into wedges

Put all the ingredients into the slow cooker, cover with the lid and cook on high for 1 hour, or on low for 3 hours.

Transfer the sauce mixture to a food processor and blitz until smooth. The sauce can be stored in an airtight container in the refrigerator for up to a week.

When ready to serve, heat up the sauce in a saucepan and serve over breadcrumbed seitan or tofu, along with some salad – thin matchsticks of carrot, cucumber, radish and chilli work really well, scattered with sesame seeds – plus some rice and lime wedges.

**SERVES 4**
**Preparation time 15 minutes**
**Cooking time 1½–2 hours**

# WHOLE SPICED CAULIFLOWER

1 large cauliflower, leaves
   removed
2 tablespoons extra virgin
   olive oil
2 garlic cloves, grated
finely grated zest and juice of
   1 unwaxed lemon, plus extra
   zest and wedges to garnish
2 tablespoons tahini
1 tablespoon za'atar
1 tablespoon sesame seeds
1 teaspoon ground sumac
1 teaspoon ground cumin
½ teaspoon ground turmeric
salt and pepper

*To serve*
fresh herbs, such as coriander
   and/or dill
pomegranate seeds
hummus

Cut a thin slice off the bottom of the cauliflower so that it will sit flat in the slow cooker pot.

Use 1 tablespoon of the oil to grease the slow cooker pot.

Put the remaining tablespoon of oil and all the other ingredients into the slow cooker and stir together well until you have a smooth paste. Dip the cauliflower into the paste, rubbing it all over, working it into all its nooks and crannies.

Sit the cauliflower in the slow cooker pot and season well with salt and pepper. Cover with the lid and cook on high for 1½–2 hours until the cauliflower is easily pieced with a fork.

Serve immediately, sprinkled with more salt, lemon zest, some fresh herbs and pomegranate seeds, along with some hummus and lemon wedges.

**SERVES 4**
Preparation time 15 minutes
Cooking time 2¾ hours

# LOADED SWEET POTATOES

4 sweet potatoes, scrubbed and
   halved lengthways
2 tablespoons extra virgin
   olive oil
1 tablespoon ground cumin
400 g (13 oz) ready-made or
   homemade vegan chilli
1 red pepper, cored, deseeded
   and chopped
salt and pepper

*To serve*
small bunch of fresh coriander,
   finely chopped
1 avocado, cut into small cubes
3 spring onions, finely sliced

Score the cut surfaces of the sweet potatoes in a cross-cross pattern. Coat all over with the oil, cumin and salt and pepper.

Lay a large sheet of foil in the slow cooker pot. Sit the sweet potatoes on the foil, bring the sides of the foil together over the potatoes and fold over to seal tightly. Cover with the lid and cook on high for 2 hours.

Unwrap the foil and top each sweet potato half with a few tablespoons of the chilli and a sprinkle of chopped red pepper. Reseal the foil, replace the lid and cook, still on high, for a further 45 minutes.

Serve warm, topped with the coriander, avocado and spring onions.

SERVES 4
**Preparation time 15 minutes**
**Cooking time 2¾ hours**

# THAI GREEN CURRY

3 tablespoons vegan Thai green
   curry paste
400 ml (14 fl oz) can coconut
   milk
2 aubergines, cut into wedges
1 red pepper, cored, deseeded
   and thinly sliced
2 tablespoons soy sauce
1 teaspoon sugar
1 red chilli, halved lengthways
   (optional)
6 makrut lime leaves
200 g (7 oz) green beans,
   trimmed
225 g (7½ oz) can bamboo
   shoots, drained

*To serve*
large handful of Thai
   basil leaves
large handful of fresh
   coriander leaves
1 lime, cut into wedges
white rice

Fry the curry paste in a saucepan over a medium heat for about 1 minute until fragrant. Add half the coconut milk and stir until the paste has dissolved. Simmer for 3–4 minutes.

Transfer the curry paste mixture to the slow cooker and add the remaining coconut milk, the aubergines, red pepper, soy sauce, sugar, chilli (if using) and lime leaves. Cover with the lid and cook on high for 2 hours until the aubergine is almost tender.

Stir in the green beans and bamboo shoots, replace the lid and cook, still on high, for a further 45 minutes.

Remove the red chilli and lime leaves. Serve immediately with the Thai basil, coriander, lime wedges and rice.

SERVES 4–6
Preparation time 20 minutes, plus soaking
Cooking time 3 hours

# BEETROOT & SWEET POTATO GRATIN

2 tablespoons extra virgin
olive oil

50 g (2 oz) cashew nuts, soaked
in cold water overnight or
in boiling water for 1 hour,
then drained

2 garlic cloves, grated

2 tablespoons nutritional yeast

1 tablespoon white wine vinegar

250 ml (8 fl oz) hot vegan
bouillon stock

400 g (13 oz) large beetroots,
peeled and thinly sliced

400 g (13 oz) sweet potatoes,
peeled and thinly sliced

2 thyme sprigs, leaves picked

salt and pepper

Grease the slow cooker pot with 1 tablespoon of the oil.

Blend together the cashew nuts, garlic, nutritional yeast and vinegar in a blender until you have a smooth paste, adding a splash of water to loosen if necessary. Stir into the hot stock in a jug and set aside.

Arrange the vegetable slices in concentric circles in the slow cooker pot – you can either lay the slices flat or sit them upright, depending on the look you like.

Pour the stock mixture over the vegetable slices, sprinkle with most of the thyme leaves and season to taste with salt and pepper. Place a tea towel or kitchen paper underneath the slow cooker lid, cover the cooker and cook on high for 2½ hours.

Remove the lid and tea towel or kitchen paper and cook uncovered, still on high, for a further 30 minutes.

Serve immediately, sprinkled with the remaining thyme leaves.

**SERVES 4–6**
Preparation time 35 minutes
Cooking time 1½–1¾ hours

# WILD GARLIC & PEA RISOTTO

*For the risotto*
3 tablespoons olive oil
2 banana shallots,
    finely chopped
½ large or 1 small leek, trimmed,
    cleaned and finely chopped
pinch of salt
300 g (10 oz) arborio rice
200 ml (7 fl oz) white wine
    or vermouth
900 ml (1½ pints) hot vegan
    bouillon stock
2 teaspoons sea salt flakes
200 g (7 oz) frozen peas

*For the wild garlic & pea purée*
100 g (3½ oz) frozen peas,
    blanched in boiling water for
    2 minutes, drained and rinsed
    under cold water
large handful of flat leaf parsley,
    plus extra, roughly chopped,
    to garnish
large handful of wild
    garlic leaves
finely grated zest and juice of
    1 unwaxed lemon, plus extra
    zest to garnish
4 tablespoons extra virgin
    olive oil
salt and pepper
grated Parmesan-style vegan
    cheese, to serve

Heat the oil for the risotto in a saucepan over a medium heat. Add the shallots and leek with the pinch of salt and sauté for 5 minutes until softened and beginning to colour. Add the rice and toss to coat, then turn up the heat to high and cook, stirring regularly, for 2 minutes until lightly toasted.

Add the white wine or vermouth and allow it to bubble up and reduce until there is no liquid visible in the pan. Transfer to the slow cooker and add the hot stock and sea salt. Cover with the lid and cook on high for 1¾ hours, stirring once halfway through cooking, until the rice has absorbed most but not all of the liquid and is cooked but still firm to the bite. However, check for doneness after 1½ hours and thereafter at frequent intervals until ready. If it seems too dry, add a splash of water.

Once the risotto is cooked, turn off the slow cooker, add the peas and re-cover, while you make the wild garlic and pea purée. Blitz together all the purée ingredients in a food processor until smooth, adding 1–2 tablespoons of water if necessary. Check and adjust the seasoning.

Stir the purée through the risotto and serve immediately, scattered with grated Parmesan-style vegan cheese and garnished with chopped parsley and lemon zest.

# MAINS:
# MORE THAN
# 3½ HOURS

**SERVES 4**
Preparation time 20 minutes
Cooking time 10 hours

# FRENCH ONION SOUP WITH MUSTARDY EMMENTAL CROUTONS

........................................................................................................................

100 g (3½ oz) butter

2 tablespoons olive oil

875 g (1¾ lb) white onions, sliced

1 teaspoon sea salt

1.5 litres (2½ pints) vegetable stock

150 ml (¼ pint) white wine

2 tablespoons balsamic vinegar

3 thyme sprigs

pepper

chopped thyme, to garnish

*For the croutons*

1 baguette, cut into 8 x 1 cm (½ inch) slices

olive oil, for drizzling

25 g (1 oz) Dijon mustard

100 g (3½ oz) Emmental cheese, grated

Put the butter and oil into the slow cooker, turn on to low and leave until the butter begins to melt. Add the onions and salt and mix together until the onions are well coated. Cover with the lid and cook for 4 hours until the onions are soft, tender and caramelized, stirring occasionally to ensure the onions are not sticking to the pot.

Pour in the stock, wine and balsamic vinegar and add the thyme, replace the lid and cook, still on low, for a further 6 hours until the soup is reduced and full of flavour. Season to taste with salt and pepper.

When ready to serve, preheat the grill. Drizzle the baguette slices with a little oil, then cook under the grill until lightly toasted on each side. Spread each slice with a thin layer of the mustard.

Ladle the soup into 4 heatproof bowls, then top each one with 2 slices of the toasted baguette and sprinkle liberally with the grated cheese. Place the bowls under the grill and cook for 3–5 minutes until the cheese has melted and is bubbly and golden.

Serve immediately, sprinkled with chopped thyme.

**SERVES 4**
Preparation time 30 minutes
Cooking time 6¾–8¾ hours

# MUSHROOM & WALNUT COBBLER

2 tablespoons olive oil

1 onion, chopped

2 garlic cloves, chopped

250 g (8 oz) flat mushrooms, peeled and quartered

250 g (8 oz) chestnut mushrooms, quartered

1 tablespoon plain flour

200 ml (7 fl oz) red wine

400 g (13 oz) can chopped tomatoes

150 ml (¼ pint) vegetable stock

1 tablespoon redcurrant jelly

2–3 thyme sprigs

salt and pepper

*For the walnut topping*

200 g (7 oz) self-raising flour, plus extra for dusting

50 g (2 oz) butter, diced

50 g (2 oz) walnut pieces, chopped

75 g (3 oz) Cheddar cheese, grated

1 egg, beaten

4–5 tablespoons milk

Heat the oil in a frying pan, add the onion, garlic and mushrooms and fry, stirring, for 5 minutes or until just turning golden.

Stir in the flour, then mix in the wine, tomatoes and stock. Add the redcurrant jelly, thyme and salt and pepper and bring to the boil. Pour into the slow cooker pot, cover with the lid and cook on low for 6–8 hours.

When almost ready to serve, make the topping. Put the flour and butter in a bowl, then rub in the butter with your fingertips until fine breadcrumbs form. Stir in the walnuts, cheese and salt and pepper. Add half the egg, then mix in enough milk to make a soft dough.

Knead lightly, then roll out the dough on a lightly floured surface until 2 cm (¾ inch) thick. Stamp out 8 rounds with a 6 cm (2½ inch) plain biscuit cutter, re-rolling trimmings as needed. Stir the mushroom casserole, then arrange the scones, slightly overlapping, around the edge of the dish. Cover and cook on high for 45 minutes or until well risen. Carefully remove the slow cooker pot from the cooker using oven gloves, brush the tops of the scones with the remaining egg and brown under a grill, if liked.

**SERVES 4**
Preparation time 30 minutes
Cooking time 6 hours 10 minutes

# ROOT VEGETABLE PUFF PASTRY PIE

1 red onion, chopped

2 carrots, chopped

2 parsnips, chopped

1 sweet potato, peeled
and chopped

2 floury potatoes (such as Maris
Piper), peeled and chopped

3 garlic cloves, crushed

1 tablespoon thyme leaves

2 tablespoons plain flour

750 ml (1¼ pints) vegetable
stock

75 ml (3 fl oz) double cream

100 g (3½ oz) frozen peas

1 tablespoon wholegrain
mustard

1 egg, beaten

1 sheet puff pastry

salt and pepper

steamed greens, to serve

Put the chopped vegetables, garlic and thyme into the slow cooker, then sprinkle over the flour and season well with salt and pepper. Toss the vegetables until well coated in the flour. Pour in the stock and stir together until well combined and there are no lumps of flour. Cover with the lid and cook on low for 6 hours.

Stir in the cream, frozen peas and mustard, replace the lid and cook, still on low, for a further 10 minutes until the sauce is thickened and creamy and the vegetables are tender.

Preheat the oven to 200°C (400°F), Gas Mark 6. Carefully spoon the vegetable mixture into a 23 x 33 cm (9 x 13 inch) ovenproof dish. Brush a little of the beaten egg around the top edges of the dish, then drape over the pastry sheet, pressing the edges to seal. Trim off any excess pastry, then brush the top with the remaining beaten egg.

Bake in the oven for 10 minutes until the top is golden brown and puffed up. Serve with steamed greens.

**SERVES 2**
**Preparation time 10 minutes**
**Cooking time 4 hours**

# SUN-DRIED TOMATO & OLIVE-STUFFED MUSHROOMS

4 portobello mushrooms
2 garlic cloves, crushed
1 tablespoon ready-made
   vegetarian basil pesto
50 g (2 oz) mascarpone cheese
4 sun-dried tomatoes,
   finely chopped
8 pitted black olives,
   finely chopped
20 g (¾ oz) vegetarian Italian
   hard cheese, grated
1 tablespoon chopped parsley,
   to garnish
mixed salad leaves, to serve

Brush the mushrooms clean and remove the stalks. Place each mushroom, gill side up, on a square of foil large enough to allow the edges of the foil to fold upwards over the mushrooms to create 'tent' parcels.

Mix together the garlic, pesto, mascarpone, tomatoes and olives in a small bowl. Spoon equal amounts of the mixture into each mushroom and smooth the tops. Sprinkle over the grated cheese.

Fold up and seal the foil over each mushroom, then place the parcels in the slow cooker. Cover with the lid and cook on low for 4 hours until the mushrooms are tender but still holding their shape.

Carefully remove the parcels from the slow cooker, then the mushrooms from the foil and garnish with the chopped parsley. Serve with a mixed salad – these are particularly good with a rocket or watercress salad.

SERVES 4
Preparation time 25 minutes
Cooking time 6 hours

# BLACK BEAN CHILLI TACOS

2 tablespoons olive oil
2 red onions, chopped
3 garlic cloves, crushed
1 teaspoon smoked paprika
1 teaspoon ground cumin
1 cinnamon stick
1 teaspoon chipotle paste
2 x 400 g (13 oz) cans chopped
   tomatoes
grated zest and juice of
   1 unwaxed lime
2 x 400 g (13 oz) cans black
   beans, drained and rinsed
salt and pepper

*For the mango salsa*
1 ripe mango, peeled
   and chopped
1 small red onion, finely chopped
¼ cucumber, finely chopped
2 tablespoons chopped
   fresh coriander
1 red chilli, deseeded and
   finely chopped
juice of 1 lime

*To serve*
8 mini flour tortillas
1 ripe avocado
1 lime, cut into wedges, plus
   a little extra lime juice
small handful of fresh coriander,
   roughly chopped
soured cream

Heat the oil in a large frying pan, add the onions and fry over a medium-low heat for 5 minutes until soft and translucent, then stir in the garlic, paprika, cumin and cinnamon and fry for a few minutes until fragrant. Transfer the mixture to the slow cooker and add the remaining chilli ingredients. Season with salt and pepper and mix together until well combined.

Cover with the lid and cook on low for 6 hours until the sauce has reduced and thickened and the flavours have developed. Remove the cinnamon stick before serving.

Make the salsa about 15 minutes before the end of the chilli cooking time. Mix together all the ingredients in a bowl and set aside.

When ready to serve, warm the tortillas in a preheated oven according to the packet instructions. Halve and stone the avocado, then remove the peel and cut the flesh into slices, squeezing over a little lime juice to stop them turning brown.

Top the warmed tortillas with the chilli, mango salsa, avocado slices, chopped coriander and a drizzle of soured cream. Serve with the lime wedges for squeezing over.

SERVES 6–8
Preparation time 45 minutes, plus cooling
Cooking time 4½ hours

# CONFIT TOMATO TART

500 g (1 lb) block shortcrust
    pastry
flour, for dusting
2 tablespoons olive oil
3 large onions, thinly sliced
1 tablespoon balsamic vinegar
2 tablespoons soft brown sugar
100 g (3½ oz) goats' cheese
    log with rind on, cut into
    thin slices
salt and pepper
thyme leaves, to garnish

*For the confit tomatoes*
1 kg (2 lb) mixed-colour
    cherry tomatoes
10 garlic cloves, peeled
a few rosemary and
    thyme sprigs
2 teaspoons sea salt
375 ml (13 fl oz) olive oil

Put the cherry tomatoes, garlic, herbs, salt and oil into the slow cooker and mix together well. Cover with the lid and cook on low for 4 hours until the tomatoes are soft, tender and wrinkled. Carefully remove the slow cooker pot from the cooker using oven gloves and leave to cool (the confit mixture can be stored in an airtight container or sterilized jar in the refrigerator for up to 2 weeks).

Roll out the pastry on a lightly floured work surface, then use to line a 20 cm (8 inch) fluted tart tin. Chill in the refrigerator for 10 minutes. Preheat the oven to 180°C (350°F), Gas Mark 4. Line the case with baking paper, fill with baking beans and bake in the oven for 10 minutes. Remove from the oven and carefully lift out the paper and beans, then return to the oven and bake for a further 5 minutes until lightly golden and chalky to the touch. Leave to cool.

Meanwhile, heat the oil in a large frying pan, add the onions and a pinch of salt and fry over a low heat for about 15 minutes until very soft and golden brown. Stir in the vinegar and sugar and cook for a further 5 minutes until the onions are caramelized and all the liquid has been absorbed. Leave to cool slightly.

Increase the oven temperature to 200°C (400°F), Gas Mark 6. Spread a layer of the caramelized onions over the base of the baked pastry case. Using a slotted spoon, add a layer of the confit tomatoes, ensuring not to add too much oil. Top with the goats' cheese, drizzle with a little of the confit oil and season with pepper. Bake for 10 minutes until warmed through. Serve sprinkled with thyme leaves.

SERVES 4
Preparation time 35 minutes
Cooking time 6 hours

# GREEK AUBERGINE & TOMATO STEW

4 tablespoons olive oil

1 red onion, sliced

2 celery sticks, sliced

3 garlic cloves, crushed

2 aubergines, cut into 3 cm
(1¼ inch) chunks

2 x 400 g (13 oz) can chopped
tomatoes

400 g (13 oz) can chickpeas,
drained

100 ml (3½ fl oz) red wine

2 tablespoons tomato purée

1 tablespoon red wine vinegar

1 teaspoon sugar

1 preserved lemon, finely sliced

salt and pepper

*To serve*

1 tablespoon toasted pine nuts

50 g (2 oz) feta cheese,
crumbled

2 tablespoons chopped parsley

grated zest of ½ unwaxed lemon

saffron rice or another grain, or
crusty bread and salad

Heat 2 tablespoons of the oil in a large frying pan, add the onion and celery and fry over a medium heat for 5–8 minutes until softened, then stir in the garlic and fry for 3 minutes until softened. Transfer the mixture to the slow cooker.

Heat the remaining oil in the pan, add the aubergine chunks, in batches, and cook over a medium heat for a few minutes on each side until golden. Add to the slow cooker.

Put the remaining ingredients into the slow cooker, season well with salt and pepper, then mix well. Cover with the lid and cook on low for 6 hours until the sauce is thick and the aubergines are soft.

Spoon into serving bowls, then sprinkle over the toasted pine nuts, feta, parsley and lemon zest. Serve with saffron rice, or couscous or any other grain to soak up all the delicious juices, or with crusty bread and salad.

**SERVES 2**
**Preparation time 15 minutes**
**Cooking time 7 hours**

# STUFFED ACORN SQUASH WITH JEWELLED WILD RICE

200 g (7 oz) cooked wild rice

40 g (1½ oz) dried cranberries

3 spring onions, chopped

40 g (1½ oz) pine nuts

2 tablespoons chopped parsley, plus extra to garnish

2 tablespoons chopped mint leaves, plus extra to garnish

2 tablespoons olive oil

1 acorn squash (or 1 butternut squash with top and bottom removed), halved horizontally and deseeded

1 teaspoon ras el hanout

salt and pepper

pomegranate molasses, to serve (optional)

Mix together the cooked rice, cranberries, spring onions, pine nuts and chopped herbs in a bowl. Add 1 tablespoon of the oil and season well with salt and pepper.

Drizzle the remaining oil over the squash halves and sprinkle over the ras el hanout, then rub the spice and oil all over the flesh using your hands. Season well, then spoon the rice mixture into the centre of each squash half.

Place 2 cookie cutters in the bottom of the slow cooker pot to create trivets (alternatively you can make trivets out of scrunched up foil), then carefully lower the squash halves on top of each trivet so they don't topple over. Cover with the lid and cook on low for 7 hours until the squash is tender.

Serve sprinkled with a little more chopped parsley and mint and drizzled with a little pomegranate molasses, if liked.

**SERVES 6**
**Preparation time 40 minutes**
**Cooking time 4 hours**

# CAULIFLOWER, CHICKPEA & APRICOT TAGINE

1 whole cauliflower
2 tablespoons olive oil
1 teaspoon cumin seeds
2 onions, sliced
4 garlic cloves, crushed
1 teaspoon ras el hanout
1 teaspoon ground cinnamon
1 teaspoon ground coriander
400 g (13 oz) can chopped
  tomatoes
1 teaspoon tomato purée
400 g (13 oz) can chickpeas,
  drained
125 g (4 oz) ready-to-eat dried
  apricots, chopped
10 green olives, pitted
  and halved
grated zest of ½ unwaxed lemon
400 ml (14 fl oz) water
100 g (3½ oz) fresh spinach
  leaves
salt and pepper

*To serve*
handful of fresh coriander,
  chopped
handful of toasted flaked
  almonds
herbed couscous

Preheat the oven to 190°C (375°F), Gas Mark 5. Cut the cauliflower into florets, reserving the outer leaves. Put the florets and leaves on a baking sheet and drizzle over 1 tablespoon of the olive oil, then sprinkle with the cumin seeds and season with salt and pepper. Roast for 15 minutes, then remove the leaves and set aside. Return the florets to the oven and continue to cook for 15 minutes until roasted and lightly golden. Set aside.

Meanwhile, heat the remaining oil in a large frying pan, add the onions and a pinch of salt and fry over a medium-low heat for 5 minutes until softened and lightly golden. Stir in the garlic and dried spices and fry for a few minutes until fragrant.

Transfer the onion mixture to the slow cooker and add the chopped tomatoes, tomato purée, chickpeas, apricots, olives and lemon zest. Pour in the measured water, then mix together.

Cover with a lid and cook on low for 4 hours until the sauce is thickened and the vegetables are tender, adding the cauliflower florets (reserving the leaves) 30 minutes before the end of the cooking time.

Turn off the slow cooker, then stir in the spinach. Replace the lid and leave to wilt in the residual heat.

Season to taste, then sprinkle with the coriander and almonds before serving with the roasted cauliflower leaves and herbed couscous.

**SERVES 4**
**Preparation time 20 minutes**
**Cooking time 4 hours**

# VIBRANT BEETROOT CURRY

.................................................................................................................................

3 tablespoons rapeseed oil

6 curry leaves

1 teaspoon mustard seeds

1 teaspoon cumin seeds

1 onion, finely sliced

4 garlic cloves, crushed

1 green chilli, deseeded and
    finely chopped

1 tablespoon tomato purée

650 g (1 lb 7 oz) fresh beetroot,
    peeled and cut into wedges

300 ml (½ pint) water

1 teaspoon salt

400 ml (14 fl oz) can coconut
    milk

*To serve*

cooked basmati rice

naan

natural yogurt with a little
    chopped mint stirred through

Heat the oil in a frying pan until hot, add the curry leaves and fry for 1 minute until they sizzle. Stir in the mustard and cumin seeds and fry for 1–2 minutes until they begin to pop, then reduce the heat to medium-low, add the onion, garlic and chilli and fry for about 5 minutes until the onion has softened.

Transfer the onion mixture to the slow cooker, add the tomato purée, beetroot, measured water and salt and mix well. Cover with the lid and cook on high for 2 hours.

Stir in the coconut milk, replace the lid and cook, still on high, for a further 2 hours until the sauce has thickened and the beetroot is tender.

Serve with fluffy basmati rice, naan and cool mint yogurt.

SERVES 4
Preparation time 25 minutes
Cooking time 5 hours 10 minutes

# SMOKED TOFU LAKSA

2 red Thai chillies, deseeded
    and chopped
1 thumb-sized piece of fresh root
    ginger, peeled and chopped
4 garlic cloves, chopped
1 teaspoon curry powder
4 small shallots, chopped
1 lemon grass stick, tough
    outer leaves removed
    and stalk chopped
10 g (¼ oz) fresh coriander,
    leaves and stalks separated
1 teaspoon smooth peanut
    butter
400 ml (14 fl oz) can coconut milk
1 litre (1¾ pints) vegetable stock
1 carrot, chopped
½ butternut squash, peeled,
    deseeded and chopped into
    3 cm (1¼ in) cubes (you want
    about 100 g/3½ oz squash)
300 g (10 oz) mangetout
4 baby pak choi, halved
    lengthways
400 g (13 oz) rice noodles
200 g (7 oz) smoked tofu, cubed

*To serve*
¼ cucumber, cut into long,
    thin strips
handful of bean sprouts
black sesame seeds
lime wedges

Put the chillies, ginger, garlic, curry powder, shallots, lemon grass, coriander stalks and peanut butter into a food processor and process to form a smooth paste.

Transfer the paste to the slow cooker, then pour in the coconut milk and stock and add the carrot and squash. Stir, cover with the lid and cook on low for 5 hours until the vegetables are tender.

Turn off the slow cooker and leave to cool slightly, then whizz the soup while still in the slow cooker pot using a stick blender. Alternatively, carefully transfer the soup to a blender and blend, in batches if necessary, until smooth.

Return the soup to the slow cooker, add the mangetout and pak choi, replace the lid and cook on high for 10 minutes until tender. Meanwhile, cook the rice noodles according to the packet instructions, then drain and set aside.

To serve, stir the smoked tofu pieces through the soup. Divide the rice noodles between 4 serving bowls, then ladle over the soup and tofu. Top with the cucumber strips and bean sprouts. Sprinkle over the black sesame seeds and serve with lime wedges for squeezing over.

SERVES 4–6
Preparation time 25 minutes
Cooking time 7–8 hours

# VEGAN BOLOGNESE

3 tablespoons olive oil
1 onion, finely chopped
1 celery stick, finely chopped
1 large carrot, finely chopped
1 garlic clove, finely chopped
25 g (1 oz) dried porcini
    mushrooms, crumbled
    or roughly chopped
150 ml (¼ pint) boiling water
300 g (10 oz) chestnut
    mushrooms, finely chopped
50 g (2 oz) dried red lentils
50 g (2 oz) dried green lentils
400 g (13 oz) can chopped
    tomatoes
1 tablespoon tomato purée
3 thyme sprigs, leaves picked
2 teaspoons Marmite
1 tablespoon balsamic vinegar,
    or more to taste
300 ml (½ pint) hot vegan
    bouillon stock
salt and pepper

*To serve*
450 g (14½ oz) dried spaghetti
grated Parmesan-style
    vegan cheese
fresh basil leaves

Heat the oil in a large frying pan over a medium-low heat, add the onion, celery and carrot with a pinch of salt and sauté for 5–10 minutes until beginning to soften and colour. Add the garlic and sauté for a further minute.

Meanwhile, put the porcini mushrooms into the slow cooker, pour over the measured boiling water and leave to soak.

Transfer the onion mixture to the slow cooker and add all the remaining ingredients, seasoning lightly with salt and pepper. Cover with the lid and cook on low for 7–8 hours. Check and adjust the seasoning, perhaps adding a dash more vinegar if needed.

When ready to serve, cook the spaghetti in a large saucepan of salted boiling water according to the packet instructions. Drain and toss with the sauce. Serve immediately, with some Parmesan-style vegan cheese grated over, garnished with a few basil leaves.

**SERVES 4**
**Preparation time 30 minutes**
**Cooking time 7 hours**

# SLOW-COOKED CAPONATA

4 tablespoons extra virgin
  olive oil
2 large aubergines, cut into 2 cm
  (¾ inch) cubes
2 celery sticks, finely sliced
2 red onions, finely sliced
4 garlic cloves, finely sliced
400 g (13 oz) can plum tomatoes
3 tablespoons sherry vinegar
1 tablespoon light brown
  soft sugar
50 g (2 oz) black olives
50 g (2 oz) raisins
3 tablespoons capers in
  brine, drained
salt and pepper

*To serve*
large handful of basil leaves
toasted pine nuts

Heat 3 tablespoons of the oil in a large frying pan over a medium-high heat, add the aubergines and sauté for 3–5 minutes until beginning to soften and colour. Transfer to the slow cooker.

Heat the remaining tablespoon of oil in the frying pan, add the celery and onions and sauté for 5–8 minutes until translucent and lightly golden brown. Stir in the garlic and cook for a further minute.

Transfer the celery and onion mixture to the slow cooker and add the tomatoes, squeezing them between your hands to break them up, the vinegar and sugar. Season well with salt and pepper. Cover with the lid and cook on low for 6 hours until all the vegetables are very tender.

Stir in the olives, raisins and capers, replace the lid and cook, still on low, for a further hour until well reduced.

Check and adjust the seasoning, then serve immediately, sprinkled with the fresh basil leaves and toasted pine nuts.

**SERVES 8**
**Preparation time 20 minutes**
**Cooking time 6–8 hours**

# CLASSIC TOMATO SOUP

2 tablespoons olive oil, plus
   extra for drizzling
1 kg (2 lb) tomatoes,
   roughly chopped
1 carrot, finely chopped
1 red pepper, cored, deseeded
   and finely chopped
3 garlic cloves, halved
1 tablespoon sugar (optional)
500 ml (17 fl oz) hot vegan
   bouillon stock
2 bay leaves
2 thyme sprigs
2 basil sprigs, plus extra leaves
   to garnish
salt and pepper
croutons, to serve (optional)

Put the oil, tomatoes, carrot, red pepper, garlic, sugar, if using, and hot stock into the slow cooker. Add the bay leaves and herb sprigs and season well with salt and pepper. Cover with the lid and cook on low for 6–8 hours until the vegetables are very tender and the soup mixture smells strongly aromatic. (You can cook the soup on high for 3 hours if you want to enjoy it sooner.)

Use an immersion blender to blend the soup mixture until smooth and creamy, or leave it to cool and blitz in a food processor. Alternatively, mash with a potato masher to a chunky purée.

Reheat the soup if necessary and serve immediately, garnished with basil leaves and black pepper, drizzled with olive oil and sprinkled with croutons, if you like.

**MAKES 2 LITRES (3½ PINTS) BROTH**
Preparation time 20 minutes
Cooking time 4–6 hours

# AROMATIC PHO

1 onion, halved

1 whole piece of fresh
   root ginger, peeled
   and halved lengthways

1 carrot, peeled and
   halved lengthways

3 garlic cloves, peeled
   and bashed

1 celery stick, halved
   lengthways

8 dried shiitake mushrooms

1 teaspoon sugar

1 teaspoon salt

2 star anise

1 lemon grass stalk, bashed

1 cinnamon stick

1 teaspoon black peppercorns

1 teaspoon coriander seeds

1 teaspoon fennel seeds

2 tablespoons soy sauce

2 litres (3½ pints) cold water

*To serve*
noodles
marinated tofu
fresh vegetables
Sriracha hot sauce
handful of fresh coriander

Heat a frying pan over a high heat until searing hot. Add the onion and ginger halves cut side down and cook until charred.

Transfer the charred onion and ginger to the slow cooker and add all the remaining ingredients. Cover with the lid and cook on low for 4–6 hours.

Strain through a fine sieve or muslin and serve hot with dried pho noodles or other noodles of your choice, cooked separately according to the packet instructions, tofu and vegetables such as pak choi (quartered and either charred before adding or poached for a few minutes in the broth), sliced spring onions and red chillies. Sriracha hot sauce and fresh coriander sprigs will provide extra punches of flavour.

**SERVES 4**
Preparation time 25 minutes
Cooking time 8 hours

# SPICED AUBERGINE WITH POMEGRANATE & FLATBREAD

3 tablespoons olive oil
1 onion, finely chopped
3–4 garlic cloves, finely chopped
2 teaspoons ground cinnamon
1 tablespoon cardamom pods,
    crushed, seeds removed
    and ground
2 teaspoons cumin seeds,
    ground
1 teaspoon ground turmeric
2 aubergines, cut into 2 x 4 cm
    (¾ x 1½ inch) wedges
2 x 400 g (13 oz) cans chopped
    tomatoes
1 tablespoon pomegranate
    molasses
1 tablespoon sugar
salt and pepper

*To serve*
ready-made crispy shallots
handful of fresh herbs, such
    as parsley, mint, dill and/or
    coriander, chopped
pomegranate seeds
flatbreads, warmed
flaked almonds, toasted
    (optional)

Heat the oil in a frying pan over a medium heat, add the onion and sauté for about 8–10 minutes until soft and translucent. Stir in the garlic and spices and cook for 1 minute.

Transfer the onion mixture to the slow cooker and add all the remaining ingredients. Cover with the lid and cook on low for 8 hours, checking occasionally and adding a splash of water if the stew looks dry.

Season the stew to taste with salt and pepper and serve, sprinkled with the ready-made crispy shallots, fresh herbs and pomegranate seeds, with warmed flatbreads on the side. Some toasted flaked almonds scattered over make a tasty addition too.

**SERVES 6–8**
Preparation time 20 minutes
Cooking time 7–9 hours

# TOFU TIKKA MASALA

2 x 400 g (13 oz) cans
  chopped tomatoes
2 tablespoons coconut oil
4 garlic cloves, finely chopped
  or grated
20 g (¾ oz) fresh root ginger,
  peeled and finely grated
6–8 cardamom pods (use black
  cardamom if available,
  otherwise green is fine)
2 cinnamon sticks
1 tablespoon garam masala
1 teaspoon ground cumin
½ teaspoon chilli powder
½ teaspoon ground turmeric
500 g (1 lb) silken tofu,
  drained and cut into 2.5 cm
  (1 inch) cubes
1 teaspoon dried fenugreek
  leaves (methi), crumbled
2 tablespoons sugar
200 ml (7 fl oz) coconut cream
salt and pepper

*To serve*
small handful of fresh coriander
1 lemon, cut into wedges
rice

Blitz the tomatoes in a food processor until smooth. Transfer to the slow cooker.

Heat the coconut oil in a frying pan over a medium heat, and the garlic and ginger and sauté for about 3 minutes until fragrant and golden. Stir in the cardamom pods, cinnamon sticks and ground spices and cook for a further minute.

Transfer the spice mixture to the slow cooker, cover with the lid and cook on low for 6–8 hours.

Stir in the tofu cubes, fenugreek leaves, sugar and coconut cream, replace the lid and cook on high for 1 hour.

Season to taste with salt and pepper and serve immediately, sprinkled with the coriander leaves and with lemon wedges for squeezing over, along with rice on the side.

**SERVES 4**
Preparation time 20 minutes
Cooking time 6¼ hours

# ALL THE GREENS SOUP

.........................................................................................................................................................

2 tablespoons coconut oil
1 shallot, finely sliced
4 garlic cloves, grated
20 g (¾ oz) fresh root ginger,
   peeled and grated
2 celery sticks, finely sliced
1 large head of broccoli,
   broken into florets and
   stalks roughly chopped
2 courgettes, roughly chopped
500 ml (17 fl oz) hot vegan
   bouillon stock
1 teaspoon ground turmeric
1 teaspoon ground coriander
400 g (13 oz) kale or spinach,
   any tough stalks removed
finely grated zest and juice of
   1 unwaxed lime
1 tablespoon soy sauce

*To garnish*
coconut cream
large handful of fresh
   coriander leaves
black and white sesame seeds

Heat the coconut oil in a frying pan over a medium heat, add the shallot, garlic and ginger and sauté for 3 minutes until fragrant.

Transfer to the slow cooker and add the celery, broccoli, courgettes, hot stock, turmeric and ground coriander. Cover with the lid and cook on low for 6 hours. (You can cook the soup on high for 2–3 hours if you want to enjoy it sooner.)

If using kale, stir in, replace the lid and cook, still on low, for a further 15 minutes until wilted and tender. If using spinach, simply stir through for about 5 minutes until just wilted.

Use a stick blender to blitz the soup until smooth, adding some water if you prefer a thinner consistency. Season to taste with the lime zest and juice, and the soy sauce.

Serve immediately, garnished with a swirl of coconut cream and the coriander leaves, sprinkled with black and white sesame seeds.

**SERVES 4–6**
Preparation time 1 hour, plus soaking
Cooking time 4 hours 40 minutes–5 hours
  40 minutes

# MUSHROOM, LEEK & THYME PIE

2 tablespoons sunflower or
    vegetable oil
2 large leeks, trimmed, cleaned
    and sliced
500 g (1 lb) button mushrooms,
    halved
4 garlic cloves, finely chopped
2 thyme sprigs, leaves picked,
    plus extra leaves to garnish
200 g (7 oz) cashew nuts,
    soaked in cold water
    overnight or in boiling water
    for 1 hour, then drained
500 ml (17 fl oz) hot vegan
    bouillon stock
2 tablespoons nutritional yeast
1 teaspoon miso paste
finely grated zest and juice of
    1 unwaxed lemon
1 sheet of vegan puff pastry
1 tablespoon dairy-free milk,
    to glaze
salt and pepper

Heat the oil in a large frying pan over a medium heat, add the leeks and mushrooms and sauté for 10 minutes until the leeks are softened and the mushrooms are beginning to colour. Stir in the garlic and thyme leaves and cook for a further minute. Transfer to the slow cooker.

Blitz the cashew nuts, hot stock, nutritional yeast, miso paste and lemon zest and juice in a food processor or blender until smooth and creamy. Pour over the leek and mushroom mixture and stir to combine. Season with pepper, and salt if needed. Cover with the lid and cook on low for 4–5 hours until the sauce has thickened and the mushrooms are very soft. Add a splash of water or dairy free milk if the mixture seems too stiff.

Preheat the oven to 190°C (375°F), Gas Mark 5. If your slow cooker pot is ovenproof, remove it from the cooker, top with the sheet of puff pastry, trim the excess around the edge and crimp to secure. Use a pastry brush to brush the pastry with the dairy-free milk to glaze and bake in the oven for 30–40 minutes until the pastry is golden brown. Alternatively, transfer the filling to an ovenproof dish, then top with the pastry, glaze and bake in the same way.

Serve immediately, sprinkled with the extra thyme leaves.

**SERVES 4**
Preparation time 25 minutes
Cooking time 6 hours

# PULLED JACKFRUIT BURGERS

2 tablespoons sunflower or
    vegetable oil
1 onion, finely sliced
400 g (13 oz) can young
    jackfruit, drained and rinsed
300 ml (½ pint) vegan cider
150 ml (¼ pint) tomato ketchup
50 ml (2 fl oz) soy sauce
50 ml (2 fl oz) apple cider
    vinegar
50 g (2 oz) dark brown
    soft sugar
1 teaspoon ground ginger
½ teaspoon cayenne pepper
1 teaspoon smoked paprika
½ teaspoon freshly grated
    nutmeg
2 teaspoons garlic powder
salt and pepper
4 burger buns, halved and
    toasted, to serve

*For the slaw*
200 g (7 oz) mixed red and white
    cabbage, shredded
1 carrot, peeled and cut into
    fine matchsticks
2 spring onions, finely sliced
finely grated zest and juice of
    1 unwaxed lime
2 tablespoons sunflower oil

Heat the oil in a frying pan over a medium heat, add the onion and sauté for about 8 minutes until softened and lightly golden. Add the jackfruit and cook for a further 5 minutes.

Transfer the jackfruit mixture to the slow cooker and add the remaining ingredients, seasoning well with salt and pepper.

Cover with the lid and cook on low for 6 hours until the jackfruit pulls apart easily with 2 forks.

Meanwhile, mix together the cabbage, carrot and spring onions for the slaw in a bowl. Whisk together the lime zest and juice and oil, pour over the vegetables and toss to coat.

Shred the jackfruit mixture and serve immediately in toasted burger buns, topped with the slaw.

**SERVES 4–6**
**Preparation time 20 minutes**
**Cooking time 6 hours**

# SPICY STUFFED PEPPERS

4–6 large peppers, any colour
   or a mixture
125 g (4 oz) quinoa
200 g (7 oz) can black beans,
   drained and rinsed
200 g (7 oz) can sweetcorn
   kernels, drained and rinsed,
   or frozen and defrosted
200 g (7 oz) passata
   (sieved tomatoes)
1 garlic clove, grated
1 tablespoon chipotle paste
2 teaspoons ground cumin
1 teaspoon sweet
   smoked paprika
salt and pepper

*To serve*
small handful of fresh coriander
sliced avocado
1 lime, cut into wedges

Slice the stalks and tops off the peppers and discard. Use a teaspoon or small serrated knife to remove the cores and seeds, taking care not to cut through the pepper flesh. Add 2 cm (¾ inch) of water to the slow cooker pot and arrange the peppers upright in the pot so that they fit snugly together.

Mix all the remaining ingredients together in a large bowl and season with salt and pepper. Spoon the filling evenly into the pepper shells, cover with the lid and cook on low for 6 hours until the quinoa is cooked through and the pepper shells have softened.

Serve immediately sprinkled with coriander leaves, along with avocado slices, and lime wedges for squeezing over.

**SERVES 4**
Preparation time 20 minutes
Cooking time 4–5 hours

# VEGETABLE GOULASH

1 tablespoon sunflower oil
1 onion, chopped
250 g (8 oz) swede, diced
250 g (8 oz) carrots, diced
250 g (8 oz) potatoes, diced
1 red pepper, cored, deseeded
    and diced
2 celery sticks, sliced
150 g (5 oz) closed cup
    mushrooms, halved
1 teaspoon smoked paprika, plus
    extra to garnish (optional)
¼ teaspoon dried chilli flakes
1 teaspoon caraway seeds
1 tablespoon plain flour
400 g (13 oz) can chopped
    tomatoes
300 ml (½ pint) hot vegan
    bouillon stock
2 bay leaves
salt and pepper

*To serve*
150 ml (¼ pint) vegan
    soured cream
plain boiled rice

Heat the oil in a large frying pan, add the onion and fry, stirring, until softened. Add the vegetables, fry for 1–2 minutes, then stir in the paprika, chilli flakes and caraway seeds and cook for 1 minute.

Stir in the flour, then mix in the canned tomatoes and stock, add the bay leaves and a little salt and pepper and bring to the boil. Transfer to the slow cooker pot and press the vegetables below the surface of the liquid. Cover with the lid and cook on high for 4–5 hours or until the root vegetables are tender.

Stir the goulash and discard the bay leaves. Spoon on to plates and top with spoonfuls of vegan soured cream and a sprinkling of extra paprika, if liked. Serve with plain boiled rice.

# SWEET
# TREATS

**SERVES 4**
Preparation time 15 minutes
Cooking time 3 hours 10 minutes

# POMEGRANATE & STAR ANISE POACHED PEARS

4 firm, ripe pears
600 ml (1 pint) pomegranate
   juice
400 ml (14 fl oz) red wine
1 tablespoon pomegranate
   molasses
1 cinnamon stick
2 star anise
1 teaspoon vanilla bean paste
   or 1 vanilla pod
1 tablespoon caster sugar
toasted chopped nuts or fresh
   pomegranate seeds, to serve

Peel the pears, keeping them whole and retaining the stalks. Put into the slow cooker and add the remaining ingredients. Cover with the lid and cook on low for 3 hours until the pears are cooked through and tender.

Carefully remove the slow cooker pot from the cooker using oven gloves, then remove the pears with a slotted spoon and set aside. Remove the cinnamon stick, star anise and vanilla pod, if using. Carefully pour the cooking liquid into a small saucepan and simmer for about 10 minutes until reduced and syrupy.

Drizzle the poached pears with the syrup and top with toasted chopped nuts or fresh pomegranate seeds. You can eat them by themselves, or serve with ice cream, crème fraiche or yogurt.

SERVES 4
**Preparation time 20 minutes, plus chilling**
**Cooking time 2½–3½ hours**

# CRÈME CARAMELS

**butter, for greasing**
**125 g (4 oz) granulated sugar**
**125 ml (4 fl oz) water**
**2 tablespoons boiling water**
**2 eggs**
**3 egg yolks**
**400 g (13 oz) can full-fat
    condensed milk**
**125 ml (4 fl oz) semi-skimmed
    milk**
**grated rind of ½ small lemon**

Lightly butter 4 metal individual pudding moulds, each 250 ml (8 fl oz).
Pour the sugar and measured water into a small saucepan and heat
gently, stirring occasionally until the sugar has completely dissolved.

Increase the heat and boil the syrup for 5 minutes, without stirring,
until the syrup has turned golden, keeping a watchful eye as it cooks.
Take the pan off the heat, add the boiling water and stand well back.
Tilt the pan to mix and, when bubbles have subsided, pour into
the pudding moulds, tilting them so that the syrup coats the base
and sides.

Put the eggs and egg yolks into a bowl and whisk together with a fork.
Pour the condensed milk and fresh milk into a saucepan, bring to the
boil, then gradually beat into the egg mixture until smooth. Strain back
into the pan, then stir in the lemon rind.

Pour the custard into the syrup-lined pudding moulds, then transfer
the moulds into the slow cooker pot. Cover the top of each one with
a square of foil. Pour hot water around the moulds so that the water
comes halfway up the sides, then cover with the lid and cook on low
for 2½–3½ hours or until the custard is set with just a slight wobble
in the centre. Lift out of the slow cooker pot with a tea towel, cool,
then transfer to the refrigerator for 3–4 hours or overnight to chill.

Dip the base of the moulds into boiling water for 10 seconds, loosen
the top of the custard with a fingertip, then turn out on to rimmed
plates to serve.

**MAKES 10 SLICES**
Preparation time 25 minutes
Cooking time 2 hours

# BANANA & WALNUT BREAD

75 g (3 oz) unsalted butter,
  softened, plus extra
  for greasing
100 g (3½ oz) soft brown sugar
2 large eggs, lightly beaten
3 ripe bananas, mashed, plus
  1 less ripe banana, halved
  lengthways, to decorate
  (optional)
1 teaspoon vanilla extract
225 g (7½ oz) plain flour
2 teaspoons baking powder
¼ teaspoon bicarbonate of soda
½ teaspoon fine salt
½ teaspoon ground cinnamon
½ teaspoon ground nutmeg
75 g (3 oz) walnuts,
  roughly chopped

Grease the bottom of a 900 g (2 lb) loaf tin. Cut a long strip of baking paper to fit the length and slightly above the short sides of the tin, then use it to line the tin (this makes it easier to remove the bread from the tin once baked).

Beat together the butter and sugar in a large bowl using a hand-held electric whisk until light and fluffy. Add the eggs, mashed bananas and vanilla extract and beat again until smooth and well combined.

Mix together the dry ingredients and two-thirds of the walnuts in a separate bowl, then fold into the banana mixture until the dry ingredients are well incorporated and there are no floury pockets.

Spoon the batter into the prepared loaf tin and smooth the top. Gently press the halved banana pieces, if using, into the batter, cut sides up, and sprinkle with the remaining walnuts.

Lower the tin into the slow cooker, then cover with the lid and cook on high for 2 hours, or until a metal skewer inserted into the middle of the bread comes out clean.

Carefully remove the tin from the slow cooker using oven gloves and leave the banana bread to cool in the tin. Remove using the baking paper tabs, then serve cut into slices.

**SERVES 6**
Preparation time 20 minutes, plus soaking
Cooking time 1½ hours

# DARK CHOCOLATE, PRUNE & ARMAGNAC CAKE

200 g (7 oz) soft prunes, roughly chopped
50 ml (2 fl oz) Armagnac
2 teaspoons vanilla extract
200 g (7 oz) plain dark chocolate, broken into pieces
100 g (3½ oz) unsalted butter, plus extra for greasing
4 large eggs
200 g (7 oz) caster sugar
½ teaspoon fine salt
100 g (3½ oz) ground almonds
50 g (2 oz) plain flour

*To serve*
cocoa powder
crème fraîche

Put the prunes into a shallow dish, then pour over the Armagnac and vanilla extract and leave to soak for a minimum of 2 hours or preferably overnight.

Melt the chocolate and butter in a heatproof bowl set over a saucepan of gently simmering water, ensuring the bottom of the bowl does not touch the water. Remove from the heat and leave to cool slightly.

Grease a 20 cm (8 inch) springform cake tin with butter and line with baking paper. Seal around the outside bottom edge with foil.

Whisk together the eggs, sugar and salt in a large bowl until pale and fluffy, then carefully fold in the melted chocolate and soaked prunes, including the liquid. Fold in the ground almonds and flour, taking care not to overmix and knock the air out. Pour the batter into the prepared cake tin.

Lower the tin into the slow cooker, then carefully pour boiling water into the pot to come about halfway up the sides of the tin. Cover with the lid and cook on high for 1½ hours until the cake is set but still has a slight wobble in the middle.

Carefully remove the tin from the slow cooker using oven gloves and transfer to a wire rack to cool the cake completely. Then remove from the tin and cut into slices. Serve dusted with cocoa powder and with dollops of crème fraîche.

SERVES 2
**Preparation time 20 minutes, plus standing & cooling**
**Cooking time 2 hours**

# EARL GREY CRÈME BRÛLÉE

.............................................................................................................................

**400 ml (14 fl oz) double cream**
**100 ml (3½ fl oz) milk**
**1 tablespoon vanilla bean paste**
**2 Earl Grey teabags**
**3 large egg yolks**
**75 g (3 oz) caster sugar, plus**
    **2 tablespoons for the crust**

Put the cream, milk, vanilla and teabags into a saucepan and warm over a medium heat until just below boiling point, then remove from the heat, cover with a lid and leave to stand for 10 minutes.

Whisk together the egg yolks and sugar in a large heatproof bowl until pale and fluffy. Remove the teabags from the milk mixture, then slowly pour over the egg yolks, whisking continuously. Pour the mixture into 2 x 9 cm (3½ inch) ramekins.

Lower the ramekins into the slow cooker, then carefully pour boiling water into the pot to come about halfway up the sides of the dishes. Cover with the lid and cook on low for 2 hours until the custard is set.

Carefully remove the ramekins from the slow cooker using a clean tea towel and transfer to a wire rack to cool. When cool enough to handle, transfer to the refrigerator and leave to cool completely for 1–2 hours or chill overnight.

When ready to serve, sprinkle a tablespoon of sugar in an even layer over each ramekin, tapping off any excess. Heat the tops using a kitchen blowtorch until the sugar is crisp and caramelized. Alternatively, place the ramekins under a preheated grill for 2 minutes until caramelized. Leave the sugar to cool and harden for a couple of minutes before serving.

**SERVES 4**
**Preparation time 30 minutes, plus cooling**
**Cooking time 2½ hours**

# BLACKBERRY & ALMOND STEAMED PUDDING

**100 g (3½ oz) butter, softened, plus extra for greasing**
**100 g (3½ oz) self-raising flour**
**100 g (3½ oz) soft brown sugar**
**2 large eggs**
**50 g (2 oz) ground almonds**
**1 teaspoon almond extract**
**1 tablespoon milk**
**vanilla custard, to serve**

***For the blackberry compote***
**300 g (10 oz) fresh or frozen blackberries**
**100 g (3½ oz) demerara sugar**
**100 ml (3½ fl oz) water**
**1 cinnamon stick**

Put all the compote ingredients into a saucepan and bubble over a low heat for 10–15 minutes until the blackberries have broken down and the mixture is thickened and jammy. Leave to cool completely, then remove and discard the cinnamon stick.

Grease a 1 litre (1¾ pint), 17 cm (6½ inch) pudding basin generously with butter. To make the sponge, put all the ingredients into a large bowl and beat together until completely combined and smooth.

Spoon the cooled compote into the prepared basin, then spoon in the sponge batter and smooth the top. Cover the basin with a piece of nonstick baking paper that has been folded with a pleat and secure with kitchen string, then cover with foil, ensuring it is well sealed. Wrap another piece of string around the basin and secure to create a string handle.

Lower the basin into the slow cooker, then carefully pour boiling water into the pot to come about halfway up the sides of the dish, under the lip of the pudding basin. Cover with the lid and cook on high for 2½ hours. Turn off the slow cooker and leave the pudding to cool slightly for about 10 minutes.

Carefully remove the pudding from the slow cooker using the string handle, remove the foil and paper, then tip out on to a serving plate. Serve with vanilla custard.

**SERVES 4**
Preparation time 25 minutes
Cooking time 1 hour

# CHOCOLATE & ESPRESSO MOUSSE

150 g (5 oz) plain dark chocolate, broken into pieces
100 ml (3½ fl oz) freshly made strong espresso, cooled
pinch of sea salt
3 large eggs, separated
100 g (3½ oz) caster sugar

*To serve*
chocolate shavings
handful of chopped pistachio nuts

Melt the chocolate in a heatproof bowl set over a saucepan of gently simmering water, ensuring the bottom of the bowl does not touch the water. Remove from the heat and leave to cool slightly, then stir in the espresso and salt.

Whisk together the egg yolks and sugar in a separate bowl with a hand-held electric whisk until pale, fluffy and voluminous. Add the melted chocolate mixture and stir until combined.

Whisk the egg whites in a clean bowl using clean beaters until medium-soft peaks form, then gently fold into the chocolate mixture until combined. Spoon the mousse into 4 x 9 cm (3½ inch) ramekins.

Lower the ramekins into the slow cooker, then carefully pour boiling water into the pot to come about halfway up the sides of the dishes. Cover with the lid and cook on high for 1 hour until just set.

Carefully remove the ramekins from the slow cooker using a clean tea towel and leave to cool slightly. Serve topped with chocolate shavings and a sprinkle of pistachio nuts. You can add a spoonful of whipped cream, if you like.

SERVES 6
**Preparation time 30 minutes, plus cooling**
**Cooking time 3½–4 hours**

# APPLE & PECAN CAKE

100 g (3½ oz) butter, plus extra
    for greasing
100 g (3½ oz) light muscovado
    sugar
75 g (3 oz) golden syrup
175 g (6 oz) self-raising flour
1 teaspoon bicarbonate of soda
1 teaspoon ground cinnamon
1 teaspoon ground ginger
2 eggs, beaten
1 dessert apple, cored and
    grated (no need to peel)
40 g (1½ oz) pecan nuts, broken
    into pieces, plus extra to serve
280 g (9 oz) cream cheese
50 g (2 oz) icing sugar, sifted,
    plus extra to decorate
½ teaspoon orange extract

Preheat the slow cooker if necessary; see the manufacturer's instructions. Butter the inside of a 15 cm (6 inch) diameter soufflé dish that is 8 cm (3¼ inches) high. Line the base with a circle of nonstick baking paper.

Heat the butter, sugar and syrup together in a saucepan over a gentle heat. Take the pan off the heat to cool slightly.

Mix the flour, bicarbonate of soda and ground spices together, then stir into the butter mixture with the beaten eggs and grated apple. Mix until smooth, then mix in the pecan nuts.

Pour into the buttered dish, cover with a dome of buttered foil and stand in the slow cooker pot. Pour boiling water into the cooker pot, around the dish so that it reaches halfway up the sides of the dish. Cover with the lid and cook on high for 3½–4 hours or until well risen and a skewer comes out clean when inserted into the cake.

Lift out the soufflé dish with oven gloves, remove the foil and leave to cool for 15 minutes. Loosen the edge of the cake, turn out on to a wire rack and peel off the lining paper. Leave to cool completely.

When ready to serve, beat the cream cheese, icing sugar and orange extract together. Transfer the cake to a serving plate, spread the icing over the top and sides of the cake and sprinkle with extra pecan nut pieces. Serve with a dusting of icing sugar.

**SERVES 6**
Preparation time 15 minutes
Cooking time 2–2½ hours

# ZESTY MARMALADE BREAD & BUTTER PUDDING

50 g (2 oz) vegan butter, plus
    extra for greasing
6 thick slices of stale bread,
    sliced diagonally in half
    into triangles
3 tablespoons marmalade
1 unwaxed orange, thinly sliced
170 g (6 oz) silken tofu
250 ml (8 fl oz) dairy-free milk
115 g (4 oz) light brown
    soft sugar
1 teaspoon vanilla bean paste
finely grated zest of
    1 unwaxed orange

*To serve*
icing sugar
dairy-free custard

Grease the slow cooker pot with vegan butter. Spread each triangle of bread with the vegan butter, on both sides, and spread the marmalade on one side of each. Arrange the bread slices in the slow cooker pot, cut edge down, so that they fit snugly together and look like mountain peaks. Nestle a slice of orange into each gap.

Blitz the tofu, dairy-free milk, brown sugar and vanilla in a food processor until smooth. Pour over the bread slices and sprinkle the orange zest on top.

Place a tea towel or kitchen paper underneath the slow cooker lid, cover the cooker and cook on high for 2–2½ hours until the bread has absorbed most of the liquid and the top is beginning to look a little golden.

Remove the slow cooker pot from the cooker using oven gloves, uncover and leave to cool slightly and firm up. Serve warm, dusted with icing sugar, along with dairy-free custard.

**SERVES 6–8**
**Preparation time 25 minutes, plus standing**
**Cooking time 3–4 hours**

# SYRUP SPONGE

........................................................................................................................................

85 g (3 oz) vegan butter, plus
    extra for greasing
75 g (3 oz) golden syrup
140 ml (4¾ fl oz) soya milk
½ tablespoon apple cider
    vinegar
85 g (3 oz) caster sugar
1 teaspoon vanilla bean paste
175 g (6 oz) self-raising flour
1 teaspoon baking powder
½ teaspoon salt
finely grated zest of
    1 unwaxed lemon
dairy-free custard, to serve

Grease a 1 litre (1¾ pint) pudding basin liberally with vegan butter, pour in the golden syrup and set aside.

Mix together the soya milk and vinegar in a small bowl and leave to curdle for about 10 minutes.

Put the vegan butter, sugar and vanilla into the bowl of a stand mixer fitted with the whisk attachment, and whisk together until pale and fluffy, or whisk with a hand whisk in a bowl.

Mix together the remaining ingredients in a separate bowl. Fold into the sugar and butter mixture half at a time, alternating with the curdled soya milk half at a time, until all the ingredients are combined and no dry patches remain and you have a smooth batter.

Pour the batter into the pudding basin. Top a sheet of foil with one of greased nonstick baking paper, fold together in a narrow pleat down the centre and place, greased side down, over the basin. Secure around the basin rim with a long length of string. Pass the string over the top of the basin and tie to the other side to create a handle. Put the pudding basin into the slow cooker. Pour in enough boiling water to come halfway up the sides. Cover with the lid and cook on high for 3–4 hours until a skewer inserted into the middle comes out clean.

Use the handle to lift the pudding basin out of the cooker, peel back the foil and paper and leave to stand for 5 minutes before turning out on to a plate to serve, with some dairy-free custard on the side.

SERVES 4–6
Preparation time 20 minutes
Cooking time 4 hours

# RHUBARB, APPLE & GINGER CRUMBLE

*For the crumble topping*
200 g (7 oz) plain flour
90 g (3¼ oz) demerara sugar
50 g (2 oz) rolled oats
1 teaspoon ground ginger
pinch of salt
160 g (5½ oz) vegan butter,
   chilled and cut into
   small cubes

*For the filling*
600 g (1¼ lb) Bramley apples,
   peeled, cored and cut into
   2.5 cm (1 inch) chunks
300 g (10 oz) rhubarb, cut into
   4 cm (1½ inch) chunks
250 g (8 oz) caster sugar
15 g (½ oz) fresh root ginger,
   peeled and grated
1 tablespoon chopped stem
   ginger in syrup
½ tablespoon cornflour
finely grated zest and juice of
   1 unwaxed lemon

Mix together all the dry ingredients for the crumble topping in a bowl. Add the vegan butter and rub in with your fingertips until the mixture resembles fine breadcrumbs. Set aside.

Put all the filling ingredients into the slow cooker and toss until well combined. Top with the crumble mixture. Lay 2 sheets of kitchen paper directly on top of the crumble. Cover with the lid and cook on low for 3½ hours until the fruit is tender.

Remove the kitchen paper, position the lid slightly ajar and cook, still on low, for a further 30 minutes until the crumble topping is crisp.

**MAKES 8–10 ROLLS**
Preparation time 25 minutes, plus resting
Cooking time 1½–2 hours

# CINNAMON TAHINI ROLLS

*For the rolls*
50 g (2 oz) vegan butter
2 tablespoons caster sugar
250 ml (8 fl oz) almond milk
7 g (about 2 teaspoons) fast-
    action dried yeast
400 g (13 oz) plain flour, plus
    extra for dusting
1 teaspoon sea salt

*For the filling*
75 g (3 oz) vegan butter
3 teaspoons ground cinnamon
1 teaspoon ground mixed spice
5 tablespoons light brown
    soft sugar
2 tablespoons tahini

*For the icing*
50 g (2 oz) icing sugar
3 tablespoons tahini
1–2 tablespoons almond milk

Melt the vegan butter, sugar and almond milk and leave to cool. Stir in the yeast and leave to stand for about 5 minutes until it starts to foam.

Put the flour and salt into the bowl of a stand mixer fitted with a dough hook, add the yeast mixture and mix until a dough forms. Continue mixing on a low speed for 3–5 minutes until smooth and springy. Alternatively, mix the ingredients together with a wooden spoon in a large bowl, then turn out onto a lightly floured surface and knead by hand for 8–10 minutes until smooth and springy. Cover with a clean tea towel and leave to rest for 10–15 minutes.

Meanwhile, mix together all the filling ingredients in a bowl.

Sprinkle the dough with a little flour and roll out on a lightly floured surface to about 30 x 40 cm (12 x 16 inches). Spread the filling over, right to the edges. Starting from a longer edge, roll the dough into a cylinder. Use a floured serrated knife to cut into 5 cm (2 inch) slices.

Line the bottom of the slow cooker with nonstick baking paper so that it comes at least 2 cm (¾ inch) up the sides. Place the rolls on their sides in the pot, spaced evenly apart. Place a tea towel or kitchen paper underneath the lid, cover and cook on high for 2 hours until the inner rolls are firm to the touch (check for doneness after 1½ hours and thereafter at frequent intervals until cooked).

Mix the icing ingredients to a spreadable consistency, adding more milk if necessary. Spread over the rolls while warm and serve immediately.

MAKES 12
Preparation time 20 minutes, plus cooling
Cooking time 1½–2 hours

# PEANUT BUTTER BLONDIE COOKIE BARS

2 tablespoons ground flaxseed
  (linseed)
4 tablespoons cold water
nonstick cooking spray or vegan
  butter, for greasing
200 g (7 oz) light brown
  soft sugar
80 g (3 oz) vegan butter
250 g (8 oz) peanut butter
1 teaspoon vanilla extract
150 g (5 oz) plain flour
¼ teaspoon baking powder
125 g (4 oz) vegan dark
  chocolate chips or
  70% cocoa vegan dark
  chocolate, chopped

Mix the ground flaxseed with the measured cold water in a small bowl and leave to stand for about 5 minutes until thickened.

Meanwhile, line the bottom of the slow cooker pot with nonstick baking paper and grease the sides with nonstick cooking spray or vegan butter.

Put the sugar, vegan butter, peanut butter and vanilla into the bowl of a stand mixer fitted with the whisk attachment and whisk together until well combined, or whisk with a hand whisk in a bowl. Add the flaxseed mixture and mix until smooth. Fold in the flour and baking powder until no dry patches remain, then fold in half the chocolate chips.

Pour the batter into the slow cooker and spread it out evenly, then sprinkle over the remaining chocolate chips. Cover with the lid, positioned slightly ajar, and cook on high for 1½–2 hours until golden around the edges and a skewer inserted into the middle comes out clean.

Uncover and leave to cool in the slow cooker pot for at least 1 hour until firmer and easier to remove. Then turn out and cut into 12 bars.

**MAKES ONE 900 G (2 LB) LOAF CAKE**
Preparation time 20 minutes, plus standing & cooling
Cooking time 2 hours

# LEMON BLUEBERRY DRIZZLE CAKE

*For the cake*
**nonstick cooking spray or vegan
   butter, for greasing**
**250 ml (8 fl oz) unsweetened
   soya milk**
**1 teaspoon apple cider vinegar**
**75 ml (3 fl oz) sunflower or
   vegetable oil**
**1 teaspoon vanilla bean paste**
**350 g (11½ oz) plain flour**
**2 teaspoons baking powder**
**1½ teaspoons bicarbonate
   of soda**
**½ teaspoon salt**
**150 g (5 oz) light brown
   soft sugar**
**2 tablespoons finely grated
   unwaxed lemon zest**
**2 tablespoons lemon juice**
**250 g (8 oz) blueberries**

*For the drizzle icing*
**100 g (3½ oz) icing sugar**
**finely grated zest and juice of
   1 unwaxed lemon**

Line the bottom and sides of a silicone or metal 900 g (2 lb) loaf tin with nonstick baking paper and grease with cooking spray or vegan butter. Ensure that the tin fits snugly inside the slow cooker (use some balls of foil to secure it if it doesn't quite reach the cooker bottom).

Mix together the soya milk and vinegar in a bowl and leave to curdle for about 10 minutes. Then add the oil and vanilla and whisk together until well combined.

Mix together all the remaining cake ingredients, except the blueberries, in a large separate bowl. Gradually fold in the soya milk mixture and blueberries until well combined.

Pour the batter into the prepared loaf tin and spread it evenly. Place a tea towel or kitchen paper underneath the lid, cover the cooker and cook on high for 2 hours until risen and firm to the touch, and a skewer inserted into the middle comes out clean.

Remove from the slow cooker and leave to cool in the tin for 10 minutes. Then use the lining paper to lift the cake out of the tin and leave it to cool completely on a wire rack. Put the icing sugar into a small bowl and use a small whisk or spoon to mix the lemon juice in gradually until you have a fairly thick icing, adding 1–2 teaspoons of water to loosen if necessary. Spread over the cake and sprinkle with the lemon zest.

SERVES 4–6
Preparation time 20 minutes, plus cooling
Cooking time 2½–3 hours

# PINEAPPLE UPSIDE DOWN CAKE

nonstick cooking spray or vegan
    butter, for greasing
50 g (2 oz) vegan butter, melted
100 g (3½ oz) light brown
    soft sugar
8–10 pineapple rings from a can,
    drained, with 50 ml (2 fl oz) of
    the syrup reserved
about 10 glacé cherries
    (1 per pineapple slice),
    without stalks
225 g (7½ oz) plain flour
200 g (7 oz) caster sugar
1 teaspoon bicarbonate of soda
½ teaspoon salt
120 ml (4 fl oz) unsweetened
    almond milk
80 ml (3 fl oz) sunflower or
    vegetable oil
1 teaspoon vanilla bean paste
1 tablespoon white wine vinegar
vegan ice cream or dairy-free
    custard, to serve

Grease the slow cooker pot with nonstick cooking spray or
vegan butter.

Pour the melted vegan butter into the slow cooker and sprinkle evenly
with the brown sugar. Arrange the pineapple rings to cover the bottom
of the pot, cutting and trimming off any excess to allow them to come
right to the sides as necessary. Place a cherry in the centre of each
pneapple ring.

Sift the dry ingredients into a large bowl and mix to combine. Add all
the remaining ingredients, including the reserved pineapple syrup, and
whisk together until you have a smooth batter.

Pour the batter over the pineapple slices and spread it out evenly.
Cover with the lid and cook on high for 2½–3 hours until a skewer
inserted into the middle comes out clean.

Remove the slow cooker pot from the cooker, uncover and leave the
cake to cool for at least 15 minutes. Upturn a serving plate over the
top of the pot and carefully flip the plate and pot together to turn the
cake out on to the plate. If your slow cooker is quite deep, find a dish
that fits snugly inside so that you can put your hand directly on the
bottom of the dish when flipping, or cut a piece of cardboard or a
cake board to size.

Serve warm or cold with vegan ice cream or dairy-free custard.

MAKES ONE 400 G (14 OZ) JAR
**Preparation time 5 minutes**
**Cooking time 5–6 hours**

# SALTED CARAMEL SAUCE

400 ml (14 fl oz) can coconut
   milk
250 g (8 oz) light brown
   soft sugar
1 teaspoon vanilla bean paste
1–2 teaspoons sea salt flakes,
   to taste
vegan ice cream

Put the coconut milk, sugar and vanilla into the slow cooker. Cover with the lid and cook on low for 2 hours. Position the lid slightly ajar and cook, still on low, for a further 3–4 hours, stirring occasionally, until the sauce turns from pale to deep brown, smells sweet and rich, and has reduced in volume. Depending on the brand of coconut milk, you may find that by the end of cooking the sauce is a little lumpy. If so, pass through a sieve or blend in a food processor until smooth.

Stir through the sea salt. Transfer to a sterilized jar, seal and store in the refrigerator for up to 2 weeks.

Serve over vegan ice cream.

# INDEX

# GLOSSARY

Aubergine ............................................. Eggplant

Baking paper ........................................ Parchment paper

Beetroot ............................................... Beet

Bicarbonate of soda ............................ Baking soda

Black beans ......................................... Turtle beans

Butter beans ........................................ Lima beans

Chickpeas ............................................ Garbanzo beans

Clingfilm .............................................. Plastic wrap

Coriander (fresh) ................................. Cilantro

Cornflour .............................................. Cornstarch

Courgette ............................................. Zucchini

Crumble (fruit) ..................................... Crisp

Desiccated coconut ............................. Dried shredded coconut

Double cream ....................................... Heavy cream

Dried chilli flakes ................................ Crushed red pepper flakes

Electric whisk ....................................... Electric beaters

Flaked almonds .................................... Slivered almonds

Flour, plain/self-raising ....................... Flour, all-purpose/self-rising

Foil ....................................................... Aluminium foil

Frying pan ............................................ Skillet

Golden syrup ....................................... Light corn syrup

Grated .................................................. Shredded

Grill ...................................................... Broil

Ground almonds ................................... Almond meal

Icing ..................................................... Frosting

Jam ....................................................... Preserves

Jug ........................................................ Pitcher

Kitchen paper ...................................... Paper towel

Mixed spice ......................................... Pie spice mix

Natural yogurt ..................................... Plain yogurt

Pak choi ............................................... Boy choy

Pastry, filo/shortcrust............................ Pastry, phyllo/basic pie dough

Pepper (red) .......................................... Bell pepper

Plain dark chocolate............................. Semi-sweet chocolate

Pudding tin ........................................... Baking mould

Rocket.................................................... Arugula

Salad leaves .......................................... Greens

Silcone muffin cases ...........................Silicone muffin liners

Spring onion.......................................... Scallion

Stem ginger........................................... Preserved ginger

Stock...................................................... Broth

Sugar, caster/icing .............................. Sugar, superfine/confectioners'

Sultanas ................................................ Golden raisins

Swede.................................................... Rutabaga

Tea towel............................................... Cloth kitchen towel

Tomato purée........................................ Tomato paste

Treacle .................................................. Molasses

# ACKNOWLEDGEMENTS

Commissioning Editor: Louisa Johnson
Photographers: Stephen Conroy, Lis Parsons, William Shaw and Eleanor Skans
Art Director: Yasia Williams
Senior Editor: Leanne Bryan
Project Editor: Vicky Orchard
Designer: Geoff Fennell
Deputy Picture Manager: Jennifer Veall
Assistant Production Manager: Allison Gonsalves